The Jesus Seminar and its Critics

ROBERT J. MILLER

The Jesus Seminar and its Critics

POLEBRIDGE PRESS

The Jesus Seminar and Its Critics

First edition

Library of Congress Cataloging-in-Publication Data

Miller, Robert J. (Robert Joseph), 1954-
    The Jesus seminar and its critics / Robert J. Miller.– 1st ed.
        p. cm.
    Includes bibliographical references and index.
    ISBN 0-944344-78-X
    1. Jesus Christ–Historicity. 2. Jesus Seminar. I. Title.

BT301.9 .M55 1999
232.9'08–dc21

99-047547

CONTENTS

ABBREVIATIONS

BCE	Before the Common Era
CE	of the Common Era
1–2 Cor	1–2 Corinthians
1–2 Chron	1–2 Chronicles
Dan	Daniel
Isa	Isaiah
John	Gospel of John
Luke	Gospel of Luke
Mark	Gospel of Mark
Matt	Gospel of Matthew
Q	Sayings Gospel Q
Sam	Samuel

PREFACE

Writing is a solitary ordeal, but no one does it alone. This book would not have been possible without the ongoing support of many.

My thanks are first due to Bob Funk and Char Matejovsky, whose trust, guidance, and assignments have encouraged and prodded me to go beyond what I thought I could do.

My colleagues and friends in the Jesus Seminar, too many to name here, have forged an extraordinary scholarly community pervaded by a spirit of collaboration which fosters an unpretentious generosity and a spirit of accountability which keeps us honest with ourselves and with the public. Without the inspiration and support I have found in the Seminar, this book would not exist.

There are three others to whom I owe especially large debts of gratitude.

Marianne Sawicki, my wife and friend, has supported my work all these years with her selfless encouragement, exegetical provocations, graceful criticism, and editorial wisdom.

From David Seeley, my colleague and mentor, I have learned more about my field than from anyone else. His intellectual integrity has shown me what is noble in the scholarly vocation. David's withdrawal from biblical scholarship is the loss of one of its finest minds.

Brian Curley, my desert partner and spiritual companion, has long sustained our search for wisdom with his courageous honesty, buoyant humor, and sage counsel. ⲱⲘⲓⲄⲄⲀⲚⲓⲤ.

The Jesus Seminar and Me

The Jesus Seminar began its work in 1985, the same year I completed my doctoral dissertation in New Testament Studies. A year later a friend invited me to attend the Seminar's fall meeting. Although I was only marginally interested in the historical Jesus, I decided to go, mostly out of curiosity. I was not prepared for what I encountered.

I had been to academic conferences before. The standard fare at these is for a scholar to read a paper, after which there is a few minutes for questions. The experience is similar to attending a lecture in a college course. There is little exchange between speaker and audience. If you want to discuss or debate anything with the speaker you must do so privately after the session. Occasionally at a conference there are panel discussions in which a few specialists make brief presentations and then talk among themselves while the audience listens. These formats reinforce the dominance of established scholars and make it difficult for new or undistinguished scholars (that is, the vast majority of them) to be taken seriously. Certainly no one cared what I thought, which was fine with me, since I never had to take a position on anything at the conferences I had attended.

A few minutes into my first session of the Jesus Seminar I could tell that it was not a typical academic meeting. There were no speakers reading papers. These had been studied beforehand and were used as the starting point for substantive discussions. Some eminent scholars were present, but did not dominate the proceedings. Everyone had their say. Honest differences were debated with both vigor and respect. This impressed me because academic debate all too often occurs in an atmosphere where the purpose seems to be to win an argument rather than to seek the truth. At the end of each session, everyone had to take a position so that we could measure our consensus: we voted. This was new to me. Not only was I challenged to make up my mind, but my decision mattered. Everyone, both the eminent and the unknown, got one vote.

I remember my mixed reactions the first time I dropped a colored bead in the voting box. It seemed a bit pretentious, even slightly irreverent. It was one thing to agree theoretically that the gospels contained both historical and non-historical material, but to make a decision about a specific passage was a bit unnerving, even though the secrecy of the vote ensured that no one would know how I voted unless I revealed it. Still, I knew that God was watching. I had been persuaded by the discussion that my vote on the first item should be black.* When the box was passed to me, even though my rational mind rejected it, I felt a twinge of guilty fear. I dropped in a gray bead.

Despite those initial jitters, I was intrigued by my first experience of the Jesus Seminar. After participating in a few more meetings I knew that it was the right place for me. I decided to make the Seminar and its projects the primary focus of my efforts as a scholar. Let me mention four reasons why I continue to participate in the Seminar.

1. *The Seminar's ethos of genuine collaboration among scholars.* Over the years I have been repeatedly impressed by the generosity with which Seminar members share their work with one another, cooperating on common projects rather than competing for individual recognition.† Those outside of academia may not know how rare this is.

2. *The Seminar's commitment to working in public.* An essential mission of the Seminar is to communicate its work to the public, an emphasis evident in our publications. Scholars generally consider this to be an optional part of their job at best or a distracting nuisance at worst. The news media has shown a fair amount of interest in the Seminar, for which we have been roundly criticized by some scholars (though I often detect a whiff of envy in their critique). In keeping with the public face of the Seminar, our meetings are open to all rather than taking place behind the closed doors of academia.

3. *The Seminar's large-scale, holistic agenda.* At my first meeting I was surprised to learn how far-reaching the Seminar's agenda was. Its foundational project was nothing less than the historical appraisal of every saying attributed to Jesus and every story told about him in all early Christian literature. This was planned as a ten-year project. I and many others had our doubts as to whether it could be sustained over such a long time. It was, though it took twelve years.

4. *The Seminar's focus on a topic that really matters: Jesus.* Biblical scholars often devote a great deal of attention to obscure and minute topics, about which they produce detailed and erudite studies. As intellectually interesting and professionally rewarding as these pursuits may be to those few specialists who are intrigued by them, and as useful as they occasionally are to scholars who are not, they actually matter very little in the bigger scheme of things. The scholarly rite of passage, the ordeal of writing a doctoral disser-

---

* For an explanation of the colors the Seminar uses in its voting, see p. 12.

† Fellows of the Jesus Seminar agree to forego individual credit for much of the scholarly work that goes into its publications.

tation, is an extended exercise in specializing in a narrowly defined subject. When I completed by Ph.D. I didn't know in what area of my field I wanted to concentrate, but I was sure that I didn't want to specialize in trivia. The Jesus Seminar is devoted to a topic that, by anyone's measure, is immensely important, not only to the field of biblical studies, and not only to the church, but to all those who take seriously the fundamental questions about the human condition addressed by the world's great religions.

ABOUT THIS BOOK

Over the years of my involvement with the Jesus Seminar, I wrote several papers for the Seminar's deliberations on methodological issues and specific gospel passages. Some of these papers were revised for publication in *Forum*, the Seminar's academic journal.[1] In addition to these seminar papers, I also wrote essays and articles in two areas. 1) Since I was committed to the Seminar's mission of publicly communicating the fruits of biblical scholarship, I wrote some pieces introducing and explaining the work of the Seminar to general readers. 2) After the publication of the Seminar's first major report, *The Five Gospels*, a number of scholarly reviews and articles appeared that were highly critical of the Seminar and its work. Much of the criticism was severe; some of it was shrill. A good deal of it seemed to be based on misunderstanding, some of it so basic that it had to be deliberate. Some of it contained crude caricatures of the Seminar's work and personal attacks on Seminar members. Clearly the Seminar had drilled into a nerve by speaking publicly and honestly about the historical Jesus. I wrote several papers responding to these criticisms and analyzing the positions of our critics.

Between 1996 and 1998 a number of my papers in these two areas were published in various formats: a chapter in a book on the resurrection, contributions to religious periodicals for general readers, and articles in academic journals.

This book owes its origin to the initiative of Robert Funk, who noticed the thematic similarities in my individual articles and essays and encouraged me to arrange and adapt them for publication in a book. He convinced me that there were two good reasons to do so: to make them available in one place and for a wider audience. Since they deal with similar sets of issues, draw on a common set of assumptions, and embody a common perspective, anyone who would benefit from one of the articles would be likely to benefit from the others. However, the fact that they were scattered in different publications made it impossible for all but the most determined scholar to track them all down. Moreover, several of the pieces are published in academic journals found only in certain specialized libraries, which made them unavailable to general readers.

Please bear in mind that I wrote each of these essays for its own purpose. I did not write the earlier ones in anticipation of the later ones, nor the later ones to build on the earlier. I thus did not plan them to be parts of a larger work. Because they were written independently of one another, each piece stands on its own.

This book is thus a collection of essays. There are two consequences of this genre that readers should keep in mind. The first regards the shape of the book. The chapters are grouped into two parts. Introductions to each part explain how the individual chapters relate to the general topic and how they cohere with one another. The first chapter in each part (chapters 1 and 4) is of a more general nature than the rest, and so should be read before the others in that part of the book. Beyond this, however, the ordering of the chapters does not reflect an outline in which a given chapter presupposes what is before it and prepares for what comes after it.

The second consequence of the genre of this book regards its texture. Parts of some chapters make the same points as parts of others because they deal with closely related questions or similar aspects of the same topic. Bringing these essays together creates some repetitions in content. In adapting these essays to be chapters in this book I have removed many overlaps, but in some cases doing so would compromise the intelligibility or self-contained character of the chapter. I must therefore ask my readers' forbearance for these few but inevitable redundancies.

Most of the chapters in this book were originally written for the general reader, which means I have avoided scholarly jargon as much as possible and explained it when it seemed prudent to use it. It also means that I have striven to explain the relevant principles of biblical scholarship and to bring to light the important assumptions on which they rest. The two chapters that I wrote originally for a scholarly audience take more for granted but are still accessible to general readers, since they do not presume knowledge of Greek or the standard works of biblical scholarship. Conversely, I hope that biblical scholars will profit from the chapters written for general readers. I know that I have learned much from what scholars write for a general audience, especially because this kind of writing can take less for granted and so must pay close attention to principles and assumptions.

Being a biblical scholar presupposes, at minimum, the ability to read the ancient languages, an intimate knowledge of the biblical texts themselves, and an acquaintance with an array of other ancient texts. It also requires an understanding of the methods of literary, historical, and social-scientific analyses of texts as well as a familiarity with the significant contributions of biblical scholarship. Scholars take all this for granted when they speak and write to one another, which is why biblical scholarship can be so obscure (and therefore sometimes can seem so profound) to outsiders. However, most of the issues, problems, and results of scholarship on the historical Jesus, and everything truly worth knowing on this topic, can be understood by anyone who is familiar with the gospels and who is willing to do some serious reading, some hard thinking, and occasionally to scrutinize a passage of scripture. All that is needed is scholars who are willing to invest the effort to communicate clearly and honestly with this audience.

I firmly believe that biblical scholarship has a right to exist only inasmuch as it takes seriously its responsibility to contribute to the larger society that supports it, both to the religious communities for whom the Bible is sacred scripture and to the wider culture for whom it is one of the monuments of Western civilization. It is in this spirit that I offer this humble book.

Part One

The three chapters of Part One introduce historical Jesus research in general and the work of the Jesus Seminar in particular.

Chapter 1, "The Jesus Seminar and the Search for Jesus," introduces the Jesus Seminar and its work. I tell why the Seminar began, what it set out to accomplish, and how it goes about its historical assessment of the gospels. I explain the voting process by which it determines its findings. I describe how and why it produced its innovative translation of the gospels (the Scholars Version). I discuss which ancient texts the Seminar studies, giving special attention to the Gospel of Thomas, the most important gospel outside the New Testament. I provide a profile of the Seminar's members and a sketch of how its commitment to collaborative scholarship affects its work, especially how it accommodates its members' diverse approaches to historical method. Finally, I argue that the Seminar's findings on the historicity of the gospels do not tell us all we need to know about Jesus. On the contrary, these results bring into sharper focus, but do not answer, vital questions regarding the meaning of Jesus' life and teaching and how we should understand his identity.

Chapter 2, "A Primer on Historical Method," introduces some fundamental aspects of how historians go about their task. I begin by noting how little attention traditional Christianity pays to Jesus as a historical person. I explain several features of the gospels that make it difficult to find the historical Jesus in them, especially their way of blending historical memory about Jesus with religious interpretations of him. I then discuss four principles of historical research that lay the foundation for any critical assessment of the gospels: 1) historical claims need to be demonstrated; 2) historical knowledge comes in varying degrees of certainty; 3) all history must be reconstructed from incomplete evidence; 4) there is a crucial distinction between historical and religious truth.

Chapter 3, "Understanding the Findings of the Jesus Seminar," is a guide to the responsible interpretation and use of the Seminar's work. I analyze three problems that make a full understanding of its results a more complex matter than it may seem to be at first sight.

The first problem has to do with the various shades of meaning for the four colors in which the Seminar indicates its historical judgments about the sayings attributed to Jesus. While the meaning of red results is clear, black results can signify different kinds of historical conclusions. A pink color for a saying often represents a compromise among differing evaluations of its historicity. Gray results are inherently ambiguous.

Second, the differences between Jesus' sayings and his deeds add another layer of complexity to the colors. Because the stories about what Jesus did were passed on in a different way than were the reports of what Jesus said, the Seminar's assessment of the historical reliability of the gospel stories had to proceed differently than its investigation of the sayings tradition. The four-color scheme, therefore, has somewhat different significance for the deeds of Jesus than it does for his sayings.

Finally, I analyze the factors that limit our understanding of why the Seminar's votes came out the way they did: the necessity of reporting the Seminar's rationale for its votes in summary fashion, the restrictions inherent in understanding the reasons for decisions reached by a collective body, and the secrecy of the Seminar's system of voting.

CHAPTER ONE

The Jesus Seminar and the Search for Jesus

Since its inception in 1985, the Jesus Seminar has attracted a good deal of attention from scholars, the media, and the public. The Seminar has been both praised and denounced. Many in the public welcome the Seminar's work, reporting that it makes Jesus and his teachings more meaningful for them. Others respond negatively to the Seminar because it challenges beliefs they consider central to Christianity. Some scholars endorse the aims of the Jesus Seminar (though not necessarily all of its findings) because it says out loud what scholars have long kept to themselves. Other scholars criticize the Seminar on a variety of fronts, from the high road of finding fault with its methods to the low road of impugning the motives or belittling the academic credentials of its members. Some simply dismiss the work of the Seminar, accusing its members of selling out to sensationalism. Some religious leaders condemn the Seminar as anti-Christian, even blasphemous.

In 1993 the Jesus Seminar released a voluminous report on the first phase of its work, *The Five Gospels: The Search for the Authentic Words of Jesus*. A full-page ad in *The New York Times Book Review* in January 1994 announced it as "a major work that may forever change the way we view Jesus." This might turn out to be more than the usual publisher's hype. The book was listed in *Publishers Weekly Religion Bestsellers* for nine months, an impressive feat for a $30 hardback over 500 pages that gives no advice about spirituality or self-improvement and that is not about angels or family values or lost scrolls filled with secret wisdom.

The surprising success of *The Five Gospels* has raised the Seminar's hopes that it just might influence public perceptions about Jesus by providing an alternative to the unchallenged fundamentalist assumptions that pervade American discourse about the Bible. Any group of non-fruitcakes that has something new to say about Jesus is sure to attract attention and arouse curiosity. Those whose information about the Jesus Seminar comes from the national media know only what reporters and editors decide is newsworthy and many suspect there is more to the story. Those who have taken the fur-

An earlier version of this chapter appeared as "The Jesus Seminar and the Search for Words of Jesus," *Lexington Theological Quarterly* 31 (Summer 1996), pp. 103–33.

ther step of perusing *The Five Gospels* may well have their own questions about the Seminar.

I have been an active member of the Seminar since 1986. In this chapter I will describe the origins, aims, organization, and procedures of the Jesus Seminar. I will then sketch out how the Seminar's work can influence our understanding of Jesus.

Biblical scholarship is inherently traditional and conservative. Its purpose is, after all, to interpret the most influential and most sacred text in Western civilization. We study the Bible because we revere the past. Those who are trained in the academic discipline of biblical scholarship are taught to do their work in sustained dialogue with the scholarly tradition of interpretation (witness the space lavished on footnotes and bibliography in academic studies of the Bible). Every verse in our scriptures has been scrutinized and commented on hundreds of times and an astonishing variety of scholarly opinions exists on virtually every topic in the Bible. It is, therefore, exceptionally rare for any scholarly endeavor having to do with the Bible to be "unprecedented." Yet it is no exaggeration to describe the Jesus Seminar as unprecedented in biblical scholarship: unprecedented in its goals, its procedures, its accomplishments, and its impact.

The Jesus Seminar was founded by Robert Funk, a scholar of international fame and a former president of the Society of Biblical Literature. Two frustrations motivated him to establish the Seminar. The first was scholarly silence on what may be called the "data base" for the historical Jesus. Scholars have published numerous studies of the historical Jesus, but without disclosing the full range of evidence on which their studies are based. No scholar prior to the Jesus Seminar has published a work in which he or she lists which specific sayings and deeds of Jesus in the gospels he or she considers historical and which unhistorical. Scholars discuss the key passages on which they base their major theses, but the bulk of the material in the gospels is passed over in silence. Unless an author "comes clean" on the data he uses for his historical reconstruction of Jesus, it can be difficult to evaluate the validity of his reconstruction. Hence, works on the historical Jesus have often seemed highly subjective and leave the impression that historical judgments about Jesus are often based on religious commitments or personal preferences.

No doubt some of this silence reflects scholarly cowardice. Despite the unprecedented intellectual freedom enjoyed by those who study religion today, few biblical scholars will admit publicly that they believe that parts of the gospels are unhistorical, and even fewer seem willing to identify specific passages as such. However, a more mundane obstacle to scholars' laying all their historical cards on the table is the sheer magnitude of the task. To study every verse in the gospels and make a responsible historical judgment about each one would be the work of a lifetime for an individual. But a group of scholars working in collaboration can accomplish this task in about a decade. The results of a project like this would have the additional advantage of transcending the inevitable idiosyncrasies of works produced by individual scholars. These considerations laid the foundation for Funk's idea of the Jesus Seminar.

The second frustration that led to the Jesus Seminar is the failure of biblical scholars to educate the public about the historical Jesus. The historical-critical approach to the Bible is taught in all mainline Christian seminaries and in all colleges and universities that teach about religion, except for schools controlled by fundamentalist or some evangelical churches. Scholars using the historical-critical approach have known for over a century that the gospels are a blend of historical remembrance and Christian interpretation, which means that not every deed and word attributed to Jesus in the gospels can actually be traced to him. Biblical scholars presuppose this in writings addressed to their peers. Yet almost no one, professors and clergy alike, tries to communicate this way of understanding Jesus to the public. The vast majority of Christians, including those in Catholic and mainline Protestant churches, are surprised, even stunned, when they hear a scholar or clergyperson assert that the gospels are part fact and part fiction. The Jesus Seminar aims to bridge the gap between scholars and the public by communicating the results of its historical study clearly, honestly, and in terms understandable to a lay audience.

HOW THE JESUS SEMINAR WORKS

The foundational goal of the Jesus Seminar was to assess the historicity of everything attributed to Jesus in all Christian sources from the first three centuries. This goal was pursued in two phases: first the words of Jesus, then his deeds. The first phase began in 1985 and was more or less complete by 1991. The results of this phase of the Seminar's work were published in 1993 in *The Five Gospels: The Search for the Authentic Words of Jesus*. The second phase was completed in 1997 and its results published the following year in *The Acts of Jesus: The Search for the Authentic Deeds of Jesus*.

At the very outset of its work the Seminar had to make two decisions: how to reach conclusions and how to communicate them to the public. On the first issue the Seminar decided that it would arrive at conclusions by voting. While voting obviously cannot decide the truth of things, it is a simple and easily understood means of reaching a conclusion when there is not unanimity. It is also a traditional method in biblical studies for achieving results in group projects. The United Bible Society's critical edition of the Greek New Testament is produced by experts who vote on various manuscript readings of the Greek text. Similarly, the ecumenical translation committees responsible for the *Revised Standard Version* and *New Revised Standard Version* voted when deadlocked over how to best translate certain passages.

As for how to publish its findings, the Seminar took its inspiration from the traditional red letter editions of the New Testament, in which the words attributed to Jesus are printed in red. The idea was to produce an edition of the gospels in which only the words that Jesus "really" said would be in red. The original proposal by Robert Funk was for members to vote either red (Jesus said it) or black (Jesus didn't say it) on individual sayings. But members balked at such a stark choice and sought the means to make finer distinctions. Eventually a four-color scheme emerged that enables the Seminar to convey important nuances. Debate continued over how to interpret the colors, but the following meanings are official:

> Red Jesus undoubtedly said this or something very like it.
> Pink Jesus probably said something like this.
> Gray Jesus did not say this, but the ideas contained in it are close to his own.
> Black Jesus did not say this; it represents the perspective or content of a later or different tradition.*

Members voted by dropping colored beads in boxes, though time constraints often forced us to vote by marking ballots (which was a lot less fun). One problem inherent in voting is that there are winners and losers. In a winner-take-all voting situation, the votes of those on the "losing" side literally count for nothing. The Seminar wanted to ameliorate the win-loss aspect of voting and find a way for everyone's vote to influence the outcome. In the system adopted by the Jesus Seminar, the results of the voting are expressed in a "weighted average." This is a number determined by assigning numerical values to the colors and applying a simple mathematical formula.[1] Thus, the statement that the Seminar voted a certain saying pink, for example, means that the weighted average of the individual votes falls

---

* For a discussion of the various shades of meaning in these four colors, see pp. 47–53.

within the numerical range assigned to pink. Many votes ended with a box containing beads of all four colors and every bead contributed to the weighted average. The Seminar's use of weighted averages means that the color coding of gospel passages must be interpreted carefully.*

The Seminar met twice a year to consider items on an agenda prepared by a program committee. Certain members wrote scholarly papers on the sayings[2] or deeds to be considered. Each paper concluded with a recommendation for voting. These papers were circulated prior to the meeting and formed the basis for discussion and debate. Scholars love discussions but are notorious for postponing judgment because they want to think over every possible aspect of an issue, weigh every piece of evidence, ponder every argument, and make precise distinctions and clarifications before making up their minds. These are good intellectual habits in themselves, but they can tempt some to avoid the accountability that comes with taking a stand. If the Jesus Seminar was to finish its work before the Second Coming, it had to keep to a demanding schedule. (At boring moments during discussions, I sometimes wondered which of us would want to change any of our votes if Jesus returned to earth during one of our meetings.) Votes were therefore held at the end of each session, forcing members to focus their attention and make up their minds quickly.

Decisions reached by deadlines may be efficient, but they can also be hasty. To guard against this danger, the Seminar provided for reconsiderations. Any member could call for any item to be reconsidered at a future meeting and was given the opportunity to make a case for a different color. This happened on a few occasions and some items had their colors changed on second votes.

Another important aspect of the Seminar's procedure was the "black list." An ad hoc committee would comb through the passages on the agenda for the next meeting and draw up a list on which they believed there was already a strong consensus for a black vote. In considering each item, committee members asked themselves if they could think of any reason why anyone in the Seminar might give it a color other than black. If the committee answered "no" unanimously, the item was put on the black list. This list was circulated to the whole Seminar months before the meeting with the notice that its items would be designated black by consensus unless some member was prepared to make a case for a different color. Black lists were useful in handling nearly all the sayings in the Gnostic gospels and some of the discourse material in the Gospel of John.

* See p. 53.

A NEW TRANSLATION: THE SCHOLARS VERSION

The manner in which the Seminar reports its work aims to help people look at the gospels in a new way—literally—by printing them in its four-color format. A similar aim, to help people *hear* the gospels in a new way, motivated some members of the Seminar to launch another project: the production of an innovative translation of the gospels. This translation is known as the *Scholars Version* (SV) because it is controlled exclusively by scholars rather than by church bodies.

The primary objective of SV is to convey the informal tone and oral style of the ancient language of the gospels, which was the common (*koine*) Greek of ordinary people. Most English Bibles sound formal and solemn, in part because they are intended for use in worship, whereas the Greek of the gospels was, for the most part, the kind of language heard in the marketplace. SV strives to approximate for American readers how an ancient Greek-speaking audience would have heard the gospels. SV aspires to be both scrupulously faithful to the original and to use English that is actually spoken by ordinary Americans.

Three brief comparisons of the Scholars Version and the New Revised Standard Version give a taste of SV's distinctiveness.

> Mark 1:15
>
> NRSV   The time is fulfilled, and the kingdom of God has come near; repent, and believe in the good news.
>
> SV   The time is up: God's imperial rule is closing in. Change your ways, and put your trust in the good news!

> Mark 1:40–41
>
> NRSV   A leper came to him begging him, and kneeling he said to him, "If you choose, you can make me clean." Moved with pity, Jesus stretched out his hand and touched him, and said to him, "I do choose. Be made clean!"
>
> SV   Then a leper comes up to him, pleads with him, falls down on his knees, and says to him, "If you want to, you can make me clean." Although Jesus was indignant,[3] he stretched out his hand, touched him, and says to him, "Okay—you're clean!"

> Mark 4:9
>
> NRSV   Let anyone with ears to hear listen!
>
> SV   Anyone here with two good ears had better listen!

Work began in 1988 on draft translations of the four gospels. As the project progressed we decided to expand its scope to include other gospels, in order to make available in one volume fresh translations of all the principal texts relevant to the study of the early gospel tradition. As the list of gospels grew, additional translators were recruited, including some specialists not associated with the Seminar. The arduous process of revising and re-revising and of coordinating the work of twenty-four contributors reached its completion in 1992 with *The Complete Gospels*, which was revised and expanded in 1994. The 1994 edition contains twenty gospels, each with introductions and notes. In addition to the four New Testament gospels, there is the sayings gospel Q, the Gospel of Thomas, important Gnostic gospels (the Secret Book of James, the Dialogue of the Savior, the Gospel of Mary), the Gospel of Peter (which contains what may have been the earliest narrative of Jesus' trial, death, and resurrection), gospels about Jesus' birth and childhood (the Infancy Gospels of Thomas and James), Jewish-Christian gospels (the Gospels of the Hebrews, the Ebionites, and the Nazoreans), and others.

WHICH TEXTS DOES THE SEMINAR STUDY?

The agenda of the Seminar was to evaluate the historicity of every utterance and every deed attributed to Jesus in Christian sources from the first three centuries. 313 CE, the year the emperor Constantine put Christianity on the road to becoming the official Roman imperial religion, was chosen as an arbitrary but significant boundary. When the Seminar was still being organized, it was discovered (this may surprise you) that no inventory of all the sayings attributed to Jesus in early Christian sources had ever been compiled. Fortunately, John Dominic Crossan, co-chairman of the Seminar with Robert Funk, had already begun this task, which he completed in 1986 with the publication of *Sayings Parallels: A Workbook for the Jesus Tradition* (Fortress Press). Its inventory contains about 500 sayings (over 1500 if you count different versions of the same saying). Most of these are found in the New Testament gospels, but a significant number are in non-canonical texts.

The Seminar deliberately ignores canonical boundaries. It does so because, in principle, a document's canonical status has no intrinsic relation to its historical reliability. As it turned out, however, nearly all the items in the non-canonical gospels were voted black, with most of their contents appearing on various black lists. The one exception is the Gospel of Thomas.

THE GOSPEL OF THOMAS

Though scholars knew that a gospel attributed to the apostle Thomas had once existed, nothing else was known about it until its accidental discovery at Nag Hammadi in Egypt in 1945. This gospel consists entirely of 114 sayings attributed to Jesus, about half of which have parallels in the synoptic gospels. Early research judged Thomas to be a late compilation that drew on the New Testament gospels. This conclusion dampened interest in Thomas, for if it was late and derivative it could shed little light on the early Jesus tradition. Besides, the only text of Thomas is in Coptic,* a language few New Testament scholars can read. So Thomas received little scholarly attention until recently, when several new and important studies converged on two conclusions: that Thomas represents an independent tradition and that some of its sayings are as early, or even earlier, that those in the synoptic gospels.[4]

Impressed by these findings, the Seminar deemed Thomas to be as worthy of close and careful attention as the New Testament gospels. As the Seminar scrutinized the sayings in Thomas one by one over the course of several years, most of its members came to agree with this new understanding of this gospel. The Seminar's appraisal of Thomas' importance is reflected in the title, *The Five Gospels* (that is, Mark, Matthew, Luke, John, and Thomas). Some scholars who still regard Thomas to be late and derivative have criticized the Seminar for even considering it with the other four. Some detractors have even attributed underhanded motives to the Seminar's interest in Thomas, insinuating that the Seminar ranks Thomas on the same level as the canonical gospels in order to mount a sensationalist challenge to the authority of the Bible.

The Jesus Seminar holds Thomas and the New Testament gospels to be of equal value for understanding the origins of Christianity. However, the Seminar did not give Thomas any special treatment. It analyzed Thomas with the same methodological rigor as it did the other gospels. The Seminar found only three sayings in Thomas that it could color red: the parable of The Mustard Seed, the blessing on the poor, and the saying about God and Caesar (Thomas 20, 54, and 100). It found 31 more sayings that it colored pink. However, of these 34 red or pink sayings in Thomas, 32 are parallels to

---

* Coptic was the native language of Egypt when Christianity arrived there. Study of the Coptic text of the Gospel of Thomas shows that this gospel was originally composed in Greek and later translated into Coptic. Several sayings in Thomas also exist on papyrus scraps in Greek. Some of the sayings in the Greek fragments of Thomas differ in interesting ways from their Coptic counterparts. See *The Complete Gospels* (rev. ed.), pp. 323–29.

material in the synoptic gospels. Of the sayings in Thomas that are found nowhere else, the Seminar traced only two to the historical Jesus: the parables of The Empty Jar and The Assassin.

> The Father's imperial rule* is like a woman who was carrying a jar full of meal. While she was walking along a distant road, the handle of the jar broke and the meal spilled behind her along the road. She didn't know it; she hadn't noticed a problem. When she reached her house, she put the jar down and discovered that it was empty.
>
> —Thomas 97

> The Father's imperial rule is like a person who wanted to kill someone powerful. While still at home he drew his sword and thrust it into the wall to find out whether his hand would go in. Then he killed the powerful one.   —Thomas 98

This assessment of these two parables was a difficult one for the Seminar to make. Each parable was initially voted gray. A later reconsideration met with the same result. An unprecedented second reconsideration resulted in pink averages for both. If the Seminar is right about these fascinating and mysterious parables, these are literally "lost" teachings of Jesus, unknown to the world for sixteen centuries.

Judging from the Seminar's overall evaluation of Thomas, this gospel turns out to be a valuable source for understanding Jesus, but not in the way many had anticipated. Except for the two parables above, the only sayings in Thomas that were voted red or pink are sayings that are also found in the synoptic gospels. This means that Thomas tells us very little about Jesus that we didn't already know from the New Testament. The important contribution that Thomas makes is that it provides numerous parallel versions of sayings found in the other gospels. Studying the similarities and differences among these different versions enables us to refine our understanding of how Jesus' teachings were passed on in the early tradition.

WHO IS IN THE JESUS SEMINAR?

Participation in the Seminar is open to any biblical scholar with a Ph.D. or its equivalent. There are no other academic, religious, or ide-

---

* "Imperial rule" is the Scholars Version translation of the Greek word *basileia* (or, here in Thomas, the Coptic word *tmntero*), traditionally rendered "kingdom," usually in "Kingdom of God."

ological tests for membership and no one with the appropriate credentials has ever been turned away. The scholar members are called "Fellows" to distinguish them from non-voting "Associate" members. All the Fellows to date are white and almost all are male, reflecting the racial and gender imbalances among scholars studying the historical Jesus. Nearly all the Fellows live in North America. A few European scholars have attended some meetings by special invitation, but distance precludes their ongoing participation, although a few Fellows occasionally travel from as far away as South Africa, Australia, and New Zealand for meetings.

Many people are curious about the religious affiliations of the Fellows, but no solid information is available on this because the Seminar does not ask this question of its members. Based on my own impressions of those who participate regularly, my guess is that most belong to mainline Protestant churches. A significant minority of the Fellows are Catholic. A good number are ordained. Some have no church affiliation. A few Jews have participated. A few Fellows consider themselves non-religious.

Some Fellows are eminent New Testament scholars, but most have the modest publication records typical for college or seminary professors who are full-time teachers. Some Fellows are retired, some have new degrees. All get one vote. Unfortunately, a few prominent gospel scholars declined to participate in the Seminar because of its democratic organization, maintaining that their votes should be given more weight than those of junior scholars. In practice, it has worked out more or less this way, even though the Seminar has never considered compromising its principle of one-member/one-vote. The judgments of prominent Fellows often have considerable weight with the other members because of their wider knowledge and the persuasiveness of their arguments. Their intellectual stature pays off in their ability to influence others to vote their way, but everyone casts one vote.

Two features of the style of the Seminar's work set it apart from other academic projects. The first is the collaborative nature of the Seminar. Writing position papers often takes considerable labor and creative thinking. These papers bear the names of their authors when circulated for meetings,[5] but the Seminar's work is published in the name of the whole Seminar. Some significant votes were influenced by brilliant and original contributions in the position papers, but the Seminar gives no individual credit in its publications. For example, the commentary in *The Five Gospels* and *The Acts of Jesus* explains why the Seminar voted the way it did, but it refers only to "certain Fellows" or "some members," not to individuals by name.[6]

This collaboration fosters a generous and cooperative working environment. One extremely positive side effect is the absence of the stifling intellectual competition that sometimes mars scholarly interaction. The debate in the Seminar is frank, sometimes raucous, and occasionally heated, but I cannot remember a case in which it devolved into a clash of egos, something I have witnessed at other academic meetings. Petty sniping and verbal aggression are remarkably rare in Seminar debates, which are often leavened with self-deprecating humor. This is not because members of the Seminar are especially virtuous. Rather, it has to do with the fact that nearly everyone in the Seminar wants to stay in it and people who want to keep working together have to learn to fight fairly over honest differences.

The second unique aspect of the Seminar's work is its public venue. All our meetings are open to the public, who may attend by registering as associates members. Associates may attend special workshops and sit in on Seminar sessions. Associates do not take part in Fellows' discussions nor vote with them, though sometimes they vote among themselves out of a curiosity to compare their votes with those of the Fellows. In their papers and discussions Fellows use all the technical jargon, foreign languages, and shorthand references that facilitate their craft, but their larger goal is to explain their work to laypeople clearly and honestly, without talking over their heads and without talking down to them. At each meeting there are times for Associates to meet informally with Fellows to discuss previous sessions, and Fellows and Associates mix freely at coffee breaks, receptions, and banquets. The Seminar's aim is to demystify biblical scholarship, to make it accessible to all who are willing to invest their time and effort in learning about it.

HOW MANY ARE IN THE SEMINAR?

The population of the Seminar fluctuates. There are new members at every meeting. Some Fellows dropped out because of theological misgivings or because key votes did not go their way. Others left simply because they lost interest or had more pressing priorities. I would estimate that thirty to forty members have usually attended each meeting. More want to come but are prevented by their schedules or travel costs. If you count everyone who participated at least once, there are about two hundred Fellows.

A few Fellows have paid a heavy price for their membership in the Seminar. One Fellow was fired from his teaching position at a conservative Christian college because of his participation in the Seminar. A second Fellow lost his teaching position at an evangelical Christian college, but was never told why he was terminated. A few members have been pressured by their institutions to resign from the Seminar. One ordained member of the Seminar was formally tried for heresy by his church and was acquitted. Some Fellows remain in the Seminar despite public attacks from within their churches. Seventy-four members consented to being named in the roster of Fellows in *The Five Gospels*, seventy-nine in *The Acts of Jesus*.

THE JESUS SEMINAR AND HISTORICAL METHOD

What is the appropriate method for identifying the teachings of the historical Jesus? In other words, how can we determine whether a certain saying in the gospels originated with Jesus or whether it originated with someone else and was attributed to Jesus by early Christians? Unfortunately, there is no widespread agreement among New Testament scholars on the solution to this question. The issue of method boils down to which questions are the appropriate ones to bring to the historical investigation of the gospel texts. The lack of scholarly consensus on this issue means that different scholars may be asking very different questions about a passage in their attempts to discover whether or not it echoes the voice of the historical Jesus.

From the earliest meetings of the Jesus Seminar, participants were aware that there was little agreement among them on methodological issues. An effort to hammer out a consensus on method died quickly. Most members believed that it was a futile enterprise. Even if it had succeeded, the Fellows worried that it might become a standard of academic orthodoxy within the Seminar. Instead, it was agreed that the Seminar would proceed without a uniform historical method. Individual Fellows would make decisions about the historicity of Jesus' sayings according to whatever method each judged most appropriate.

Occasionally a Fellow would address a particular point of method relevant to the analysis of a certain saying or story in one of the Seminar's working papers. There were frequent debates about the appropriateness of various criteria of historicity. Although the Seminar did not devote sessions specifically to methodology, it was clear that some progress toward wider agreement in this area was being made as the Fellows continued their historical investigations.

When the time came to prepare the Seminar's report on the Gospel of Mark, it was apparent that there was a need for a comprehensive explanation of historical method, so as to clarify how and why the Fellows of the Seminar reached their historical conclusions. To meet this need for public accountability, Robert Funk prepared a lengthy study that analyzed the methods actually used by the Fellows and formulated them into methodological theses. Funk's study was discussed for over a year and its formulations were amended and refined. The end result of this process was the chapter on "Rules of Evidence" in *The Gospel of Mark: Red Letter Edition* (1991), which begins as follows:

> Fellows of the Jesus Seminar employ rules of evidence in determining what Jesus actually said. The rules formulated in the following essay were gleaned from the essays and debate of the Seminar over a six-year period. As a result, they are not hypothetical rules; they represent actual practice. (p. 29)

These rules and theses were later reorganized, reformulated, and elaborated with explanations and examples for the "Rules of Written Evidence" in *The Five Gospels* (pp. 16–34). Analysis of the historicity of the gospel stories that report the deeds of Jesus raises a different set of methodological issues than those raised by the historical investigation of Jesus' sayings. Robert Funk discusses the Seminar's basic approach to the assessment of the deed stories in the introduction to *The Acts of Jesus* (pp. 8–36).

THE JESUS SEMINAR AND THE HISTORICAL JESUS

The Jesus Seminar sees its work as a first step, not the last word. It is a first step in that the Seminar's goal is to invite others to take seriously questions about the historical Jesus and to provide reliable guidance toward some answers. But the Seminar's investigations are a first step in a more fundamental way. Even if everyone comes to agree with the Seminar's findings,* two supremely important questions would remain: 1) what did Jesus mean by his teachings and his deeds, and 2) who was he? Coming up with a list of authentic sayings and deeds of the historical Jesus has been a signal accomplishment, but it is really only a first step toward understanding Jesus. The list of authentic deeds allows us to see the difference between what Jesus did and what the earliest Christians made him do in their stories about him, but these deeds need to be interpreted in order for us to understand what Jesus was trying to achieve. Similarly, the list of authentic sayings enables us to distinguish his voice from the voices of his early followers,

---

* This, of course, is impossible since not even all the Fellows agree with the coloring of each passage.

but it only starts the process of understanding what message that voice was trying to communicate. The Seminar's list of sayings and deeds is the final product of one quest and the raw material for another.

What did Jesus mean?

It is important to know whether a certain saying actually comes from Jesus, but this may not tell us much about what the saying means. The Fellows discovered early on that consensus about the historicity of a saying does not always indicate agreement about its meaning. Obviously, one needs some idea about the meaning of a saying in order to judge its historicity, and the Seminar had numerous discussions about what certain sayings meant. However, unless a decision about a saying's meaning was crucial for a decision about its historicity, the Fellow chairing the session would wield the gavel and refocus the agenda. No votes were taken on the meaning of sayings.

The history of Christianity bears abundant witness that the meaning of Jesus' life and teachings is often far from obvious. Biblical scholarship has made much progress in understanding his words and deeds within their ancient context, but much remains uncertain.

Hearing what people *say* is one thing; understanding what they *mean* is quite another. Nevertheless, knowing what Jesus really said is indispensable to discovering what he meant. The Seminar's list of red and pink sayings can be the starting point for the effort to make sense of the teaching of the historical Jesus. The task is formidable, for it requires not only understanding Jesus' sayings, but more importantly, discerning how the individual teachings fit together into a coherent message. A full understanding of Jesus' message needs to take into account his deeds along with his words, to discover the connections among them, and to interpret them within the real-life context of his time and place in all of its social, economic, political, and religious dimensions. So much remains to be done. The Seminar hopes that its labor can provide a responsible foundation on which to build. By clarifying what the historical Jesus said and did, the Jesus Seminar's work can help us hear more clearly the good news about the kingdom of God that compelled and empowered the heart and mind of Jesus.

Who was Jesus?

The Seminar's work contributes to, but does not directly produce, an understanding of who Jesus was. Any historically responsible answer to this question must take into account what Jesus really said and did and distinguish that from what early Christians attributed to him and said about him. However, a list of Jesus' authentic sayings and deeds does not yield any clear answer to the question of his identity. Let me briefly discuss three traditional ways of understanding Jesus that will have to be reevaluated by anyone who takes the work of the Seminar seriously. My remarks here are only sketches, and by no means definitive. They are meant only to give some preliminary sense of what implications the findings of the Seminar might have on our understanding of the historical Jesus.

1. *Jesus claimed to be the incarnate Son of God who came to earth to save us from sin.* Belief in the divinity of Jesus arose among the first generation of Christians and was given its official formulation by the Church councils of the fourth and fifth centuries. For many Christians this belief is the essence of Christianity and the standard of orthodoxy. Since this way of understanding Jesus is so fundamental for so many Christians, it is crucial that we set it in proper perspective by recognizing that it is not a *historical description* of Jesus, but an *affirmation of belief* in his supernatural origin and divine mission. It can be neither demonstrated nor disproven by any historical evidence. In this respect, the Seminar's findings can neither affirm nor deny this belief.* What historical research can establish is whether the statements in the gospels in which Jesus claims this status and role were actually spoken by him, or were developed by early Christians and attributed to him after his death. The Seminar concluded in every case that these statements originated with the early Church.

The Jesus Seminar (and virtually all New Testament scholars who are not fundamentalists) maintains that early Christians made Jesus into the spokesman for their own beliefs about him. So, for example, all the statements in the Gospel of John that presuppose belief in Jesus' supernatural origin (for example, the "I am" statements) are colored black. There are some Christians today who accept that the historical Jesus did not claim to be God. For most of the public, however, this is news, even though it is nothing new to biblical scholars and theologians. For centuries, Christian theology established the divinity of Jesus by starting with statements in the gospels in which he claimed (or seemed to claim) to be divine. The results of twentieth-century New Testament scholarship have caused theologians who accept the historical-critical study of the Bible to abandon this approach.[7] Some in the media have sensationalized this part of the Seminar's work, characterizing it as radical, provocative, or iconoclastic. But this is so only because the Seminar is stating publicly what scholars and theologians in the mainline churches have known for decades.

---

* For a discussion of the difference between historical conclusions and religious affirmations, see pp. 42–44.

2. *Jesus claimed to be the Suffering Servant.* A second view that the Seminar's findings undermine is the belief that Jesus thought of himself as the Suffering Servant of Isaiah 53. As with the belief that Jesus was the incarnate son of God, so also here it is essential to keep in mind a crucial distinction: who Jesus was and who Jesus claimed to be are very different kinds of questions. Whether Jesus *was* the Suffering Servant of Isaiah's prophecy is a matter of religious belief and cannot be decided one way or the other by historical research. Whether Jesus *claimed* he was the Suffering Servant, however, is a historical question and so falls within the scope of the Seminar's investigation of which sayings go back to Jesus.

My impression is that very many Christians today believe that Jesus considered himself to be the Suffering Servant who was fulfilling the prophecy of Isaiah. Many Christians may be surprised to learn that this position can be supported only by a single passage in the New Testament: only once, in Luke 22:37, does Jesus quote a Suffering Servant text (Isa 53:12) and apply it to himself.[8] Some scholars have argued that there are echoes of Suffering Servant texts in Mark 10:45 and Mark 14:24,* but this was refuted some forty years ago by other scholars.[9] Since there is practically no evidence at all that Jesus saw himself as the Suffering Servant, New Testament scholars seldom discuss it. The Seminar voted unanimously to color Luke 22:37 black, a result that would surprise very few scholars. Perhaps the Seminar's attempt to bridge the gap between scholars and the public will help correct this popular misconception about the historical Jesus.

3. *Jesus claimed to be the apocalyptic Son of Man or an apocalyptic prophet.* A third result of the Seminar's work has stirred much controversy among scholars: the findings that Jesus did not proclaim that God's kingdom was coming soon, that he did not predict that the world would end during the lifetime of his early followers, and that he did not speak of his own second coming on judgment day. The view that the historical Jesus was an apocalyptic prophet gained wide scholarly acceptance early in this century and has been the prevalent opinion until recently.[†] Several important scholarly studies in the 1980s and 90s, some by Fellows of the Seminar, have challenged this view. With the Jesus Seminar adding its collective voice against the apocalyptic portrait of the historical Jesus, it is now difficult to discern what the majority opinion is among New Testament scholars.

---

* Mark 10:45: "The Son of Adam ("Son of Man" in traditional translations) didn't come to be served, but to serve, and even to give his life as a ransom for many." Mark 14:24: "This is my blood of the covenant, which has been poured out for many."

† It is interesting to note that most New Testament scholars held, and many still hold, that the central message of Jesus' teaching was a prediction that turned out to be wrong: that the Kingdom of God and the end of the world were coming within one generation.

Whether the work of the Jesus Seminar will help to bring about a new scholarly consensus on this issue is yet to be seen. Right now scholars are divided. Having collectively studied all the gospel evidence, the Jesus Seminar has decisively arrived at its position. We ask only that others, scholars and laypeople alike, consider our position, follow our reasoning, and see whether our arguments make sense historically.

CHAPTER TWO

Historical Method and the Historical Jesus

A Primer

JESUS AND THE CREEDS

Among the earliest and most reliable sources for what Christians believe are the creeds. A "creed" (from the Latin *credo*, "I believe") is an authoritative summary of official doctrine cast in the form of a personal profession of belief. Christian history has produced a number of creeds, but two of them stand out as the most important: the Apostles Creed and the Nicene Creed. Both come from the early centuries of Christianity and both are all but universally accepted as the bedrock of Christian belief. Hundreds of millions of Christians recite them in church every Sunday.

The Apostles' Creed was formulated in the second century so that Christians could give clear and uniform answers when asked what they believed. Here is the first half of it:

I believe in God the Father almighty,
Creator of heaven and earth;
and in Jesus Christ, his only Son, our Lord;
who was conceived by the Holy Spirit,
born of the virgin Mary //
suffered under Pontius Pilate,
was crucified, died, and was buried.
He descended into hell.
On the third day he rose again from the dead,
and ascended into heaven.

Many Christians are so familiar with this creed that they might not notice that there is something strange, even startling, about it: the creed goes directly from Jesus' birth to his death. (I have marked this transition with a //.) These two events are connected with the only other people named in the creed: the Jew who gave him life and the Roman who put him to death.

The second half of this chapter appeared as "Back to Basics: A Primer on Historical Method," *The Fourth R* 11.6 (November–December 1998), pp. 11, 14–17, 20. The first half of this chapter appears in print here for the first time.

These names place Jesus in a historical time and place. But the creed is totally silent about his life. To judge by the Apostles' Creed, neither anything Jesus said nor anything he did is essential to Christian faith.

The Nicene Creed is named after Nicea, the city in Asia Minor (now Turkey) where, in the fourth century and under the supervision of the Roman emperor Constantine, Christian bishops officially defined the doctrine of Jesus' divinity. This creed is longer and more elaborate than the Apostles' Creed, but it too shows no interest in the life or teachings of Jesus. Here is the first half of the Nicene Creed. (See again the jump from Jesus' birth to his death at the //.)

> We believe in one God, the Father, the Almighty,
> maker of heaven and earth, of all that is, seen and unseen.
> We believe in one Lord, Jesus Christ,
> the only Son of God, eternally begotten of the Father,
> God from God, Light from Light, true God from true God,
> begotten, not made, one in being with the Father;
> through him all things were made.
> For us and for our salvation he came down from heaven.
> By the power of the Holy Spirit he took flesh from
> the virgin Mary and became a man. //
> For our sake he was crucified under Pontius Pilate;
> he suffered, died, and was buried.
> On the third day he rose again according to the scriptures.
> He ascended into heaven.

Though virtually all churches agree with the creeds, not all Christians use them to summarize their beliefs, especially those who want to use only biblical expressions when defining the Christian faith. (The creeds of course are not found in the Bible.) When these Christians are asked to state the essential Christian affirmations about Jesus, they usually come up with a common list of beliefs, a kind of unofficial creed, expessed in more or less the following way: Jesus is the divine Son of God who came to earth in human form, was born of a virgin, died for our sins, rose from the dead, and now reigns in heaven. Again we see a statement of belief about Jesus that skips everything between his birth and his death.

It is worthwhile pondering this omission. Christianity is an extraordinarily diverse religion. Throughout its history Christians have disagreed about all kinds of things and at times disagreed so strongly that they have killed one another over some of their differences. Christians today agree on very little, yet most seem to agree that what Jesus said and did before he died is relatively unimportant for Christian faith. Only his miraculous birth and sacrificial death matter. This should strike us as odd. The creeds (both official ones like the Apostles' Creed and the Nicene Creed and the unofficial summary of belief outlined above) proclaim that God came to earth, but have nothing to say about what He said or did while He was here.

It's not that Christians ignore the life and teachings of Jesus. Far from it. Most churches read and preach from the gospels every Sunday. And extremely few Christians, if any, would say that they don't care what Jesus said and did. Nevertheless, this does not seem to be central to their faith. Judging from the creeds, one can be fully Christian without knowing anything about what Jesus taught.

Not everyone is satisfied with this situation. Many Christians want to know more about Jesus than the few statements about him in the creed. Some Christians believe that they have a personal relationship with Jesus and want to base this relationship on more than the few beliefs in the creed that they simply take on faith. Some perceive that in order to follow Jesus they have to know what he taught and what he stood for.

There are also those who for various reasons can no longer believe the creedal affirmations about Jesus, but who still are enlightened by his wisdom and inspired by his example. There are people who have never been Christian but who want to learn from one of the greatest of the world's religious teachers. There are also those who are interested in Jesus because they want to understand the foundations of Western civilization, which has been profoundly shaped by his life and teachings. People like these—Christians, post-Christians, and non-Christians alike—want to fill in the empty center in the creedal description of Jesus. They are interested in the *historical* Jesus, that is, Jesus as he was between his birth and his death. The historical Jesus cannot be discovered in the creeds. His entire life is left blank as the creeds go immediately from "born of the virgin Mary" to "suffered under Pontius Pilate." To search for the historical Jesus we must look elsewhere: in the gospels.

WHAT'S THE PROBLEM?

The search for the historical Jesus begins with the realization that we have to *search* for him. At first glance this seems to be a straightforward project: if you want to find out about Jesus, read the gospels. However, what at first seems simple turns out to be rather complicated if we read the gospels all the way through, if we read them carefully, and if we ask logical questions along the way.

For one thing, the gospels contain very little or nothing at all about important aspects of Jesus' life. They tell a great deal about his teaching and his arguments with various opponents; they narrate a few dozen of his deeds (many of them faith healings); they give very brief reports about a few key moments in his life (such as his baptism and his confrontation with the merchants in the temple); and they go into great detail about the events leading up to his death (nearly one-fifth of the material in the gospels deals with the last two days of Jesus' life). But the gospels frustrate us if we want to know about Jesus' family, his friends, his education, or his personal development. Except for a few stories about his birth and infancy and one incident in his childhood, we read nothing at all about his life before he became a public figure. (These "hidden years" of Jesus fascinate many Christians and have been a topic of extravagant speculation for centuries.) A lot of what we need to know about someone if we want to really understand him, such as his motivations, the influences on him, his emotional and psychological make-up, and how he made his key decisions, is not reported in the gospels. We are not even informed about something as basic as whether Jesus was married or had children. It seems that the gospels were not written to satisfy our curiosity about what the life of Jesus was really like.

Another, and far more serious, problem with using the gospels to learn about Jesus becomes apparent when we compare the different gospels to one another. There is a great deal of similarity among them, as we would expect. In fact, the first three gospels are so similar to one another that if a random passage from them were read aloud, in most cases only an expert biblical scholar could tell from which gospel the passage was taken. However, along with the broad similarities there are many, many differences—some minor and some major. Most passages in one gospel have parallel passages in one or more of the others. Comparing these parallel passages turns up hundreds of differences. Sometimes the differences amount to little more than a slight variations in the wording or a different emphasis, but sometimes the differences are so pronounced that they amount to inconsistencies or even contradictions among the gospels.

There is a third problem with trying to use the gospels as straightforward, factual sources of information about Jesus. This problem is less obvious than the second problem, but once you see it, you can easily grasp how important it is. People usually read the gospels a little bit at a time. But we can also read an entire gospel all the way through and study it as a whole. We can study its story line, the way it portrays Jesus and other characters, the themes it emphasizes and the ones it doesn't, and all the other aspects of that gospel that make it a significant piece of literature. This way of analyzing the gospels makes it clear that they are much more than loose collections of

Jesus' words and stories of his deeds. It shows that the gospel writers carefully organized and edited the words and deeds of Jesus in order to communicate with their own audiences. If we want to understand the messages of the gospels, we must let each one speak on its own terms. This means that we must be careful to consider only what is actually written in a specific gospel and not mentally add in what we remember from other parts of the Bible. The better we are at this, the more we are able to appreciate the distinctiveness of each gospel.

Matthew, Mark, Luke, and John do not all say the same thing, even though they use a lot of the same material. All this has profoundly important consequences. It means that the gospel writers did something more complex than simply record and hand on what they had heard and read about Jesus. It means they consciously used the words and deeds of Jesus as the raw material from which they fashioned their own distinctive understandings of the *meaning* of his words and deeds. It means they adapted, embellished, updated, edited, and interpreted their material in order to communicate new messages about Jesus that were tailored to the religious issues of their specific times and places. It means that along with the memories of what Jesus said and did we also get the evangelists' *interpretations* of what Jesus said and did, what we today might call their "spin" on Jesus. What they called it was their "good news" about him.

Looking back over these three problems we can see that our search for Jesus has to meet three challenges.

1. We have to work with what the gospels actually give us. It's not everything we want to know. It may not even be most of what we want to know. We can learn a lot, but we have to accept the fact that not all of our questions can be answered.

2. We have to read the gospels "against" one another and take seriously their differences. It may be tempting to gloss over the many disagreements and assume they don't make a real difference. But if we take the gospels on their own terms rather than try to fit them into our preconceptions, we have to respect both their similarities and their differences. In the case of important differences, we must try to determine which version gets us closer to the historical Jesus.

For example, all four gospels report that Jesus created a major disturbance in the temple—quoting scripture after knocking over the tables of the moneychangers. Matthew, Mark, and Luke narrate this incident during the last week of Jesus' life, whereas John has it in chapter two of his gospel, where it is virtually the first thing Jesus does in public. Which chronology makes more sense historically?

3. We have to be familiar with the distinctive method and message of

each gospel. This will enable us, at least partially, to distinguish material that sounds more like Jesus himself from material that reflects the spin of the evangelists.

Each of the gospels is a unique blend of historical remembrance and religious interpretation. The basic task entailed in finding the historical Jesus is to tease out the historical memories about him from the blend of memory-and-interpretation in which the Christian gospels present him. This is a formidable challenge. In order to meet it we need to know what each gospel has in common with other gospels (that is, a gospel's sources and traditions) and how each one molds its received tradition and combines it with its own unique material to fashion its distinctive portrait of Jesus.

A simple way of stating the essence of this task is to say that we need to factor out what the evangelists add to Jesus' words and deeds in order to recover the historical basis behind their presentations of him. In order to do that, we need to know how each gospel tends to shape its material and be able to detect the presence of these interpretive dynamics in any given passage. The more we know how Luke, for example, expresses himself through the words and deeds he attributes to Jesus, the better prepared we are to recognize the voice of the historical Jesus speaking throughout the words of the Lukan Jesus.

THE HISTORICAL JESUS AND THE RISEN LORD

One can see all three of the above problems right on the pages of the gospels, though it may take some careful study to appreciate them fully. There is another problem, however, that is not directly evident in the gospel texts, but comes into view when we reflect on the religious context in which they were written. This problem is simple to grasp, but its implications are complex and far-reaching. It is a problem at the heart of the search for the historical Jesus. It is this: *the gospels are written from the perspective of the belief that Jesus was raised from the dead.* Those Christians who passed on the material that would go into the gospels, the evangelists themselves, and the Christians for whom they wrote all believed that Jesus was living in heavenly glory and was actively involved in their lives. When these Christians read or talked about the words and deeds of Jesus, they were thinking not about a historical figure from their past, but rather about the supernatural Lord living in their present.

It is crucial that we understand how this belief affected the gospels and all the material that went into them. It means that historical memories of what

Jesus said or did were preserved within the framework of Christian faith in the living Lord. Christians did not think that a teaching of Jesus was important because it was something he had said to his fellow Jews in the past. When Christians heard a teaching of Jesus, it was important to them because they believed it was something Jesus was saying to them now. A telling example is the promise attributed to Jesus that "wherever two or three are gathered together in my name, I will be there among them" (Matt 18:20). This makes no sense at all as a saying by the historical, earthly Jesus, because it would put him in the impossible situation of being physically present in more than one place at one time. But it makes perfect sense as a promise of the risen Lord, who is not limited by time and space.

Examples like this one clearly indicate that, while some of the words and deeds attributed to Jesus reflect what happened in the life of the historical Jesus, others reflect Christian beliefs about the risen Jesus. This means that *the gospels are a blend of historical memories about Jesus and religious interpretations of him that arose after his death.* The gospels are faith-inspired portraits of Jesus written decades after his death by and for those who worshiped him. Some elements of these portraits are based on solid historical memories of his words and deeds. This kind of information tells us about the historical Jesus. However, some of the material in the gospels, perhaps most of it, is based on what the earliest Christians "made of" Jesus in the years after his death. This kind of information tells us not so much about Jesus as about the early Christians' faith in their lord and savior. To put it clearly and bluntly: not everything in the gospels is historically reliable.

The problem, then, in finding out what the historical Jesus said and did is that teachings and stories that reflect Christian belief that developed after Easter are attributed by the gospels to Jesus before his death.* The gospels make no clear demarcation between the historical Jesus and the risen Jesus. The early Christians were not attempting to deceive anyone by this. For one thing, the gospels were not written for outsiders; they all presuppose that their audiences are Christian.† But what is more important, the gospels put some words and deeds of the risen Jesus back into the story of his life because, *for the early Christians who told and heard these gospel stories, the risen Jesus was the same as the historical Jesus*: the teacher and healer from Galilee

---

* The final chapters of three gospels have stories about Jesus after his resurrection, but these are not the only places where the words and deeds are those of the risen Jesus, as we see from the example of Matt 18:20.

† This fact about the audiences of the gospels has important implications for how we should understand some of the stories within them. For a discussion of how this affects our assessment of resurrection stories, see pp. 137–43.

was their exalted Lord. For them there was no "problem" of the historical Jesus. Faith and history were one and the same.

HISTORY AND FAITH

History and faith may have blended together for the early Christians, but they are not the same for us. For nearly all of Christian history, Christians have believed the Bible to be historically accurate. They have done so for two basic reasons. First, the Church taught that the Bible carried God's authority, and since God certainly knew the facts of history, the Bible was historically reliable. Second, before the rise of modern science, there was no good reason to think otherwise.

However, we no longer live in that time. We all know that believing in something doesn't make it true. Because of our place in the history of our civilization, we have inherited ways of thinking that are profoundly influenced by science. We expect historical claims to be backed up by evidence, not by appeals to faith or religious authority.

What exactly do we mean by "history"? Before defining this concept we need to keep in mind that *history is a form of knowledge*. While this might seem to be a small point, or even common sense, it is actually quite important. It means that we cannot define history simply as "what happened in the past." Since history is a form of knowledge, we have to define it as "what *we know* about what happened in the past." The two words I emphasized are mutually reinforcing and need some explaining. First, history is what *we* know in that it is public knowledge, based on evidence that is available to all. We can see why this is important by considering the example of the gospel stories in which Jesus walks on water. Anyone who accepts these stories as literally true can do so only by assuming that Jesus was able to do what no one else can, i.e., walk on water. This assumption is not available to everyone because it is based on the prior belief that Jesus is the divine Son of God. Those who do not believe that Jesus is divine do not assume that he could walk on water and so do not take those stories as history, especially since they were told and written by those who believed in Jesus' divinity. Even though some Christian scholars argue that those stories are historically accurate, others can easily recognize that this conclusion is dependent on religious faith, not on public evidence.

Turning to the second emphasized word in my definition, history is what we *know* in that it goes beyond acknowledging what is merely possible or slightly probable (see Excursus One below). Historical knowledge is built out of the most plausible construals of the relevant evidence. The knowledge we attain about what happened in the past is not absolute in the sense that it totally excludes the possibility of doubt. That ideal can sometimes be attained in forms of knowledge that are highly abstract (like mathematics and logic) or that are based on simple observations of fact (like the natural sciences),* but it is not available in history (see the second principle below).

Historiography, the writing of history, is part science and part art. If we are to be responsible in our search for the historical Jesus, we first need to examine what historians try to do, how they go about it, and what they actually come up with. Since everyone who searches for the historical Jesus is acting as an historian, we need to understand something about the methods of historiography and about what historians can and cannot do. Toward this end I invite you to examine four principles of historiography, principles that are essential for understanding what we are doing when we search for the historical Jesus.

First principle

The first principle is that *you do not know it if you cannot show it.* To open up this principle we can compare historiography to two other processes which strive to get to the truth of events: journalism and the justice system. (I realize that using reporters and lawyers as examples of truth-seekers may strike many as odd, given the widespread stereotype of them as frequently playing fast-and-loose with the truth. If so, I ask you to suspend any prejudice you may harbor about the news media and the legal profession because I want to look at how these institutions ideally function.)

In one way, historians are like journalists. They are supposed to check the information they receive. If they cannot confirm it, they should report it as such. For both journalists and historians it is irresponsible to report as a fact what is only an unconfirmed report. They should also tell us *how* they got their information. We expect good journalists and good historians to collect as much relevant information as they can, to look at all sides of an issue, to tell us how reliable their information is and why, and to report and attempt to resolve discrepancies among their sources.

All these factors point to the same underlying principle: good historians and good journalists need to do more than just tell us what happened; they also need to show us what information they used, how they acquired it, and how reliable it is. Only then should we accept their version of events.

---

* Much knowledge in the natural sciences is not absolute, but a good amount is, e.g., that butterflies come from catepillars.

In another way, historians are like lawyers. They are required to prove their cases with evidence and convincing arguments. At a trial we do not believe witnesses just because they give testimony. We want to know how good their memories, vision, and hearing are and if they actually know what they're talking about. We want to know whether someone's testimony is based on first hand experience or on hearsay. We want to distinguish between what people actually witnessed and what they inferred. When we hear expert testimony, we want to know the difference between what is solidly established and what is speculation. We want to inquire into witnesses' motives. If witnesses give different versions of the same event, we want to know if the differences are serious and, if so, which version is closer to what really happened.

Another helpful analogy between historical investigation and a legal proceeding has to do with the concept of proof. A criminal trial requires a very high burden of proof: a prosecutor must show that a defendant is guilty "beyond a reasonable doubt." While some historical matters can meet this burden of proof, historical investigations are often more like a civil trial, in which a verdict of "probably true" is an acceptable outcome.

The most famous murder trial of the twentieth century is an excellent example of how this difference can work. O. J. Simpson was tried twice for the murder of Nicole Brown and Ronald Goldman. In his criminal trial he was found not guilty, whereas in his civil trial he was found liable for these deaths. Many factors undoubtedly help to explain the different outcomes, but a crucial one has to do with the much stricter burden of proof in criminal cases, as opposed to the lower standard in civil court, where a verdict can be based on a simple preponderance of the evidence. Another factor is that the jury in the civil trial was allowed to hear evidence that is not admissible in a criminal trial, such as the facts about Simpson's history of physical violence against his wife.

Knowing about the different burdens of proof and the different kinds of evidence presented in these two trials helps us understand how two juries could reach opposite conclusions. In a literal sense the jurors were charged with a historian's task: to decide, on the basis of the evidence available to them, what had happened on the night of those deaths. In evaluating the findings of historians in general, or of historical Jesus scholars in particular, it is important to ask two questions: 1) on what evidence are they basing their findings?, and 2) what standard of proof are they using in weighing the evidence?

Remember that the concept of proof in historical research applies to conclusions that are adequate for historical knowledge, which is neither perfect nor infallible. The two legal understandings of proof discussed above can serve as handy markers for imagining a spectrum of historical certainty. At the high end of this spectrum are conclusions that are beyond a reasonable doubt. At the low end are those that are based on a preponderance of the evidence. Most conclusions fall somewhere in between these two standards. Thus there are differing degrees of certainty in historical research. I suggest that a conclusion is *adequate* for historical knowledge if it falls anywhere on this spectrum. When dealing with partial evidence sometimes even our best reconstructions of past events do not yield adequate knowledge. Sometimes the evidence points in both directions. In these cases, both conscientious jurors and competent historians can legitimately draw different conclusions from the same evidence. In any case, we can responsibly evaluate a given historian's conclusions only if we know the answers to those two questions above. If we are looking at different evidence or using a different standard of proof, we may well reach different conclusions. If we are not aware that our evidence or standards differ, we will not know why our conclusions do.

Applying this to the search for the historical Jesus, we insist that if a scholar claims that certain passages in the gospels are historically accurate, he has to make his case. The same holds if he claims that a passage is historically inaccurate. The point is that claims about the historical Jesus have to be demonstrated by evidence and argument.* A crucial consequence is that no scholar whose method is truly historical can use any gospel material for a portrait of the historical Jesus unless he has demonstrated its historical reliability. Thus our first principle of historical investigation: *you do not know it if you cannot show it.* We can also put this a bit differently: *you cannot use if you do not prove it* (as long as we keep in mind the qualified meaning of *proof* discussed above).

Second principle

A second principle is that *there are no absolute certainties in history.* Historiography is a rigorous intellectual discipline, but it is not an exact science like chemistry or astronomy. While some knowledge in those sciences is educated guesswork, a great deal is absolutely certain. It is certain, for example, that water is composed of hydrogen and oxygen and that the moon orbits the earth. Anyone who doubts these simply doesn't understand. But history is seldom like this. Nearly everything in our historical knowledge is less than 100 percent certain. To illustrate this principle, consider something

---

* "Argument" doesn't mean disagreement. It is used here in its strict sense, that is, "a series of statements leading to a conclusion." In an argument one gives the reasons for a conclusion. To give an argument it is not enough to state your position; you also need to explain why you think it's true.

that no one doubts: that President Kennedy was assassinated in 1963. There is plenty of controversy over who killed him, but everyone agrees that he died from gunshot. Now suppose someone claims that John Kennedy did not die in Dallas, but recovered from his wounds and decided to withdraw from public life. So he and those around him agreed to pretend he had died. Someone else's body was put in his coffin and he still lives in secluded comfort on an isolated Pacific island. In case word of this should ever leak out and people demand that the body in the coffin be exhumed, the conspirators made arrangements for a phony examination that would confirm that the body was indeed JFK's.

This may sound crazy, but it is *possible*. Nobody can disprove it. Kennedy's assassination is as certain as anything in history can be, and there is no real reason to doubt it, but it is not certain in the way the undoubted facts of chemistry and astronomy are. In historical matters, "certainty" means something like "overwhelmingly probable with no good evidence to the contrary." To take another farfetched example, a few people believe that human beings have never been to the moon, but that all the lunar landings were filmed on a stage at a secret government installation. Such a belief cannot be disproven, but that doesn't mean that we should doubt that men have walked on the moon. However, we do have to admit that we might change our minds if Neil Armstrong were to make a confession owning up to the hoax, and other astronauts confirmed his admission.

When we deal with ancient history, there are far fewer "certainties" than with the recent past. With the historical Jesus the certainties are very few indeed. We can be certain that Jesus really existed (despite a few highly motivated skeptics who refuse to be convinced), that he was a Jewish teacher in Galilee, and that he was crucified by the Roman government around 30 CE. Everything else about him is less than certain—which means that the search for the historical Jesus is a matter of judging what is more or less probable. Because of the nature of the gospel material, we are constantly dealing with degrees of probability. Nearly all statements about the historical Jesus fall on a spectrum from "very probable" to "somewhat probable" to "somewhat improbable" to "very improbable" to "extremely doubtful." (Beyond even "extremely doubtful" there is a huge number of statements, limited only by the imagination, that are certainly false, such as the rumor that Jesus spent his early years in India learning Eastern philosophy. Statements like this are certainly false, not because they are hard to believe; some people find them easy to believe and besides, a lot of things that are hard to believe really happen. They are certainly false because they are unsupported by even a shred of credible evidence.)

EXCURSUS ONE
The Concept of Possibility

At this point we need to clarify a term that can cause trouble if it is misused: "possibility." There are different ways to define this word and, for the sake of casting the net broadly, I will use the most inclusive definition: something is possible if it involves no conceptual contradiction. A simple way of putting this is that something is possible if we can imagine it. A square circle is impossible because the concepts "square" and "circle" are mutually contradictory. We cannot form an image of a square circle. A flying elephant, strange as it may seem, is not impossible. The concepts "flying" and "elephant" are not contradictory, even though they have never come together in a real animal. But we *can* imagine it. In *fact*, elephants do not and cannot fly in our physical world, but the *concept* of a flying elephant is still possible.

Understood in this way, the concept of possibility is not very helpful in historical matters. Endless historical scenarios can be concocted, and virtually all of them are possible, even the weirdest or most fantastic. That's why to say that a certain scenario is possible almost always is to say nothing about it at all.

A final point on this matter: there are no degrees of possibility. Something is either possible or impossible, but expressions like "very possible" have no meaning. Often when people say this they really mean "probable" rather than "possible." But it's crucial to make the distinction between possibility and probability because very different criteria apply in each case. To be historically possible, something only needs to be imaginable. However, for something to be historically probable means that there is some evidence for it. Not everyone in the historical Jesus discussion seems aware of this distinction, for we often read statements like "It is quite possible that Jesus _____" or hear questions like "Isn't it possible that Jesus _____?" Fill in the blank with any scenario you like, no matter how bizarre: the answer will always be yes.

EXCURSUS TWO
Historical Truth and the Word of God

The principle that there are no absolute certainties about history runs head on into a widespread version of the traditional Christian belief in the divine authority of the Bible. This belief claims that since God is responsible for the contents of the Bible, it must be true in every way, especially historically. So if the Bible tells us that a certain event happened, then we can be sure that it did because we have it on the infallible authority of God. This belief, therefore, denies our second principle of historiography.

There are two responses that need to be considered in evaluating this very popular belief. The first is that, as we have seen, the Bible often reports the same event in different ways. A perfectly clear example comes from the Old Testament, which reports something that even people who've never opened the Bible know: David killed Goliath (1 Sam 17). It also reports, in a later and seldom read passage, that Goliath was killed, not by David, but by an obscure Israelite soldier named Elhanan (2 Sam 21:19).* Among the dozens of inconsistencies in the New Testament, we can consider the two genealogies of Jesus in Matthew and Luke, both of which trace Jesus' ancestors through Joseph, but which contradict one another as soon as they get to Joseph's father. Or we can consider Jesus' baptism. Was Jesus baptized by John the Baptist (as in Matthew and Mark), by someone else after John was imprisoned (as in Luke), or not at all (as in John)? Or we can wonder whether Mary and Joseph lived in Nazareth and Jesus was born while they were visiting Bethlehem (as in Luke), or whether they lived in Bethlehem and moved to Nazareth some time after Jesus was born (as in Matthew).

There is no need to multiply examples. Invoking God's authority to certify the literal truth of the Bible requires us to ignore what the Bible actually says. Please note: I am *not* denying the divine authority of the Bible. I am insisting that if we honor the Bible enough to respect what it really says, then we cannot claim it is literally true in every case, even if it carries God's authority. Besides, who says that God's truth can only be a literal truth?

A second response to the belief that God's authority makes the Bible a source of historical certainties is that belief in the divine authority of the Bible is just that: a belief. If people believe that a story in the Bible is historically accurate because they also believe the Bible to be the inerrant Word of God, we are still dealing with a belief. One belief does not transform another belief into a fact. To determine the historical accuracy of a story we need evidence, and a belief by itself is not evidence. For the sake of clarity, we can define "evidence" as information that is objectively and publicly verifiable, something on which competent and honest observers agree. For example, in a murder trial the gun that fired the fatal bullet is evidence. Who fired the gun may be in dispute, but if the competent witnesses agree that it is the murder weapon, then the gun is evidence. If a witness *believes*

---

* This contradiction was noticed even in ancient Israel. When the author of the books of Chronicles, who used the books of Samuel as a source, wrote his version of Israel's early history, he tried to dispel the discrepancy by asserting that Elhanan killed Goliath's *brother* (1 Chron 20:5).

it is the murder weapon, but that belief cannot be objectively verified (for example by ballistics experts), then this *belief* will not be treated as *evidence*.

In judging the historical accuracy of any report, historians rely on historical evidence. They do not simply take someone's word for it, not even if some people (or millions of people) believe that the report is backed up by God's authority. As a final example on this matter, we can consider a report about Jesus that comes from outside the Bible, in this case from the Qur'an, the scripture of Islam, which Muslims believe to be word-for-word directly from God and so unquestionably true in every respect. The Qur'an teaches that Jesus was a great prophet, but it denies that he died on a cross. It says that people thought they had crucified Jesus, but that they were mistaken.[1] What does a historian do with this report? One billion Muslims believe that Jesus did not die on a cross because they believe God says that he didn't. Obviously, however, this belief, no matter how widespread or strongly felt, cannot sway historical inquiry, which can base its judgments only on public evidence. What is the evidence for Jesus' crucifixion? It is: a) the numerous statements in the New Testament and other early Christian documents, all of which agree on this point; b) the absence of any ancient indication to the contrary; and c) corroborating reports from ancient non-Christian historians. This evidence will not convince believing Muslims that the Qur'an contains a historical error. Nevertheless, this need not prevent us from counting Jesus' death on a cross as historical knowledge, for the evidence is more than adequate. Jesus' death by crucifixion is as certain as anything in ancient history can be.

Third principle

The third principle is this: *all history is reconstruction*. The events of the past are gone forever. They can influence the present, and strictly speaking, the present is created by the lingering effects of the past. But past events in their "pastness" can exist only in memory or imagination. Since we have no memories of events earlier than our own childhoods, the historical Jesus exists *only* in our imagination. The life of the historical Jesus has to be reconstructed. It has to be pieced together from the evidence left behind, much as archaeologists reconstruct ancient buildings from the few pieces left on the ground.

The term "historical Jesus" refers to this reconstruction that exists in our imagination. It is what philosophers call a "mental construct," an image we piece together in our minds. The historical Jesus, because it is a mental construct, is not the same as the "real" Jesus, that is, Jesus as he knew himself and was known by those close to him.

Some Christian thinkers are uncomfortable with the implications of all this. They do not want the Christian religion and their own personal faith to depend on the historical Jesus, precisely because the historical Jesus is a reconstruction, which, by definition, is the result of intellectual effort and so comes with no guarantee of certainty. They want their faith to be based on truths that are certified by divine authority. Since historical inquiry cannot deliver this kind of certainty, these thinkers claim that Christian faith is based on the risen Christ, not the historical Jesus. This seems to mean that history doesn't matter to Christianity, though they seldom put it in words as blunt as this.

Luke Johnson proposes that the "real Jesus" is not Jesus as he really was in person during his lifetime, but the resurrected Jesus that Christians are supposed to experience in their lives. This definition allows Johnson to claim that, while (other) scholars are chasing unreal shadows in searching for the historical Jesus, Christian believers are in touch with the real thing. But this is really nothing more than a word game, a way of getting around the problem of history by redefining terms.*

The idea that Christian faith does not depend on the historical Jesus is common in contemporary Christian thought. But to me and many others it is an exceedingly strange idea. It means that it shouldn't matter to Christians what Jesus really said or did. However, it mattered to his disciples; why else would they have followed him? It mattered to those who killed him. It certainly mattered to Jesus. And it must matter to you because you're reading this book. The proper basis for Christian faith is a complex matter and we can leave that to theologians and philosophers to sort out. But, at a minimum, Christians simply have to care about what Jesus taught and did. And so should non-Christians who are interested in understanding religion, morality, or the foundations of Western civilization. We cannot attain the certainty we'd like, but we have to do our best. And the reconstructions that come from critical historical inquiry, if we have patience with our evidence and humility about our conclusions, are the best we can do.

Fourth principle

The final principle is that *history has nothing to say about the truth of religious beliefs.* To understand this principle we can use the example of a common Christian belief: Jesus died for our sins. Everyone agrees that Jesus died, but not everyone believes, nor can it be demonstrated either way, that his death atoned for sins. "Jesus died" is an historical statement, but "for our

---

* For an extended critique of Johnson's theories about the "real Jesus" and the irrelevance of history for Christian faith, see chapter 5.

sins" is not; it is a religious interpretation of an historical event. It does not tell what happened, but instead expresses one way of understanding the *meaning* of what happened. We can see that "Jesus died for our sins" is not an historical report as soon as we raise the question of evidence. If we were to seek evidence for this, what would it look like, and where would we look for it? Some Christians might claim that the evidence for Jesus' atonement is their own sense of being forgiven by God, but this is an internal spiritual experience that is not public evidence. It would be impossible to show, and rather strange even to try to show, that one's sins really were forgiven and that Jesus' death is what enabled that forgiveness.

"Jesus died for our sins" is a blend of historical statement and religious belief, a report of an event plus an interpretation of its meaning. Historical inquiry can verify the one but not the other. The judgment that the "for our sins" is not historical is not a judgment that it is *un*historical (or untrue)—it means that it is not in the category of history at all. That Jesus died "for our sins" is an *a*historical statement: it is neither historical nor unhistorical. It is a religious claim and so its truth must be assessed by means other than historical inquiry. Whether the doctrine of the atonement is true is something about which historians can say nothing one way or the other. Of course they may have their own religious beliefs about this, but in their capacity as historians they can neither confirm nor deny it.

Scholars need to remain aware of this distinction, since their religious beliefs can so easily influence their historical conclusions. Almost all Jesus scholars are Christians, although some identify themselves as former Christians and a few are Jewish. It is rare for a scholar to examine the historical evidence and draw conclusions that go against his or her own deeply held religious beliefs. That is why it is crucial that discussions about the historical Jesus be conducted on the basis of evidence and argument: that scholars tell us not just what they think, but why.

There are a few exceptions to the principle that history has nothing to say about the truth of religious beliefs because some of them depend on the literal truth of historical statements. If, for the sake of argument, the Qur'an were right and it were not historically true that Jesus died on a cross, then of course it would not be true that he died on a cross for our sins. To take another example, consider the statement that "Jesus was born in Bethlehem in order to fulfill prophecy." This is a combination of an historical claim about where Jesus was born and a religious belief about the purpose of his being born there. The evidence for the historical claim is mixed and historians are divided. If it could be established that he was born in Bethlehem, this would still not confirm the religious truth of the belief about its purpose.

However, if it could be established that he was *not* born in Bethlehem, it would mean that the belief that he was born there to fulfill prophecy was not true. Therefore, to the principle that history has nothing to say about the truth of religious beliefs, we need to add an exception clause: ". . . except for those beliefs that depend on the literal truth of historical statements."

We need one final clarification of this principle, and it has to do with the teachings of Jesus. The search for the historical Jesus requires sifting through the teachings in the gospels and distinguishing what he really said from what was attributed to him from a later perspective. However, the historical judgment about whether or not a certain teaching is actually from Jesus has no bearing on the religious or moral truth of that teaching. Two examples can illustrate this. It is very probable that Jesus said, "Blessed are you poor; God's kingdom belongs to you."[2] But whether the poor really are blessed is not something that historical inquiry can determine. On the other hand, the historical Jesus probably did not say, "There is more rejoicing in heaven over one sinner who repents than over ninety-nine righteous people who have no need to repent." This verse is very likely to be a later interpretation of the parable of the lost sheep that Luke added to Jesus' words.[3] However, the fact that Jesus didn't say it doesn't mean it's not true. That is an issue of theology, not history.

CONCLUSION

In summary, there are four principles of historical research that are essential for a proper appreciation of what the search for the historical Jesus is all about.

1. Claims about history have to be demonstrated by evidence and argument.
2. Historical knowledge is always a matter of greater or lesser degrees of probability; it is never absolutely certain.
3. All history is reconstruction, the result of fitting together the partial evidence so as to imagine what the past was like.
4. Findings about the historical value of biblical passages neither support nor undermine the truth of religious beliefs, except for those few beliefs that depend on the literal truth of historical statements.

All of these principles remind us that our historical knowledge has inherent limitations: it does not deliver absolute certainties; it is not discovered whole, but rather pieced together; and, except in rare cases, it cannot be used to settle questions about religious beliefs. To be sure, these limitations can be frustrating, for we naturally crave knowledge that is certain, especially when it comes to knowledge that bears on religion. Yet, without these four principles to guide the historical imagination, one runs the risks of mistaking wishful thinking for history and of attributing divine authority to one's own reconstruction of the life and teachings of Jesus.

Exchanging simplistic assumptions for the principles of critical historical research helps us to accept our historiography for what it really is, even with its limitations. And this is an essential step toward accepting our portraits of the historical Jesus for what they really are: our best informed and most honest attempts to express what we can (and cannot) know about Jesus from the imperfect evidence available to us, using the best methods we know to discipline our historical imagination.[4]

CHAPTER THREE

Understanding the Findings of the Jesus Seminar

The Five Gospels and *The Acts of Jesus* contain the full texts of the gospels with the words of Jesus or the stories about him printed in four colors.[1] Each saying, speech, or story is followed by commentary that gives a summary explanation of what the Seminar decided about its historical value. These two books thus tell what the Seminar concluded about the historicity of each gospel passage and explain the reasons for the Seminar's findings. The analysis in *The Five Gospels* and *The Acts of Jesus* is an alternative to the fundamentalism and naive literalism so entrenched in our society. These volumes meet the needs of many readers who use them as handy reference books on the historicity of the gospels. However, those who want to study these two books critically may find that it is no simple task to get beyond a superficial understanding of the Seminar's work. Three factors complicate the situation. 1) The deeds of Jesus must be analyzed differently than his sayings; the Seminar's findings about the historicity of the sayings do not have quite the same meaning as its conclusions about the stories of his deeds. 2) A closely related problem is that the Seminar's four colors can convey complex meanings; the same color can sometimes mean different things. 3) It can be difficult to figure out why some votes came out the way they did.

RED, PINK, GRAY, BLACK

Reports of what Jesus *said* and stories about what he *did* are different types of literary artifacts. Their different literary characteristics and the different kinds of information they convey means that a critical evaluation of the historical value of a saying has to be expressed somewhat differently than a judgment about the historicity of a deed. Because of this distinction, I will first discuss the meanings of the four colors as they apply to the sayings in the gospels. Then I will discuss the nuances involved in understanding the coloring of the stories about Jesus' deeds.

A much shorter version of this chapter originally appeared, along with an earlier version of chapter 1, as "The Jesus Seminar and the Search for Words of Jesus," *Lexington Theological Quarterly* 31 (Summer 1996), pp. 103–33.

Coloring the Sayings of Jesus

Here is one official definition of the meaning of the colors as they apply to the sayings in the gospels.

> Red   Jesus undoubtedly said this or something very like it.
> Pink   Jesus probably said something like this.
> Gray   Jesus did not say this, but the ideas contained in it are close to his own.
> Black   Jesus did not say this; it represents the perspective or content of a later or different tradition.[2]

The four colors serve as readily intelligible markers on a spectrum from very high confidence that an item comes from Jesus (red) to very high confidence that it comes from elsewhere and was attributed to him (black). However, being more precise about the interpretation of the colors can get tricky. Let's consider them one at a time.

Red

Anyone familiar with the historical-critical approach to the gospels will understand how rarely we can be confident that a scene or saying in the gospels reflects an exact historical memory. Our earliest literary sources draw on sayings and stories that had been transmitted orally for about forty years, by people who were interpreting them along the way. The evangelists adapt, embellish, reorganize, and rewrite what they take from their sources, and even create some of their material outright. For members of the Seminar to vote red they had to be satisfied that an item survived both the oral tradition and the process of writing the gospels without being modified in any way that matters. Because this degree of certainty is so difficult to attain, Fellows seldom voted red. Even when some red votes were cast, red results were rare because they require a strong majority of members to vote red. It only takes a small number of black votes to pull the weighted average down to pink.* I consider it a minor miracle that any saying ended up printed in red. All told, the Seminar decided on fifteen red sayings (twenty-five if you count different versions of the same saying).

Black

A black vote seems simple enough to understand, and usually it is. It means "'Jesus did not say this; this represents the perspective or content of a

---

* For an explanation of the Seminar's use of weighted averages, see p. 147, n.1.

later or different tradition." Like red results, black results represent widespread agreement. A small percentage of red or pink is enough to offset a majority black vote and average out into a gray result. But unlike red votes, black votes can express various kinds of judgments because the verdict "Jesus didn't say this" can be based on very different reasons. A black vote might reflect a certainty: this saying is inconsistent with other things I'm sure Jesus said or it reflects a situation that existed only after his death. But it might also reflect uncertainty: this saying surely reflects the perspective of the evangelist, but this *could* also be Jesus' own perspective; however, since there is no good evidence that it comes from Jesus, I vote black. In other words, if there is no good evidence connecting a saying with Jesus, many Fellows would vote black, not because they are sure he didn't say it, but because they cannot find the evidence to make even a small case that he did. This point needs to be understood clearly because it goes to the heart of how historical research must be conducted. When historians judge that an event "really happened," it means that its occurrence can be established from the available evidence. If we are to come up with an historical account that is more than wishful thinking, we can only claim to know something if we can demonstrate it from the evidence. This is the first principle of historical inquiry that I discussed in the previous chapter: you do not know it if you cannot show it.

This principle underlies many of the black votes cast by the Seminar, so let me elaborate on it. The first thing here to take seriously is the fact that the gospels are Christian writings. This may seem too obvious to point out, but it has very important consequences for historical Jesus research. Every word in the gospels *either* was derived from earlier sources (either written works or the various strands of the oral tradition) after decades of use by Christians *or* was composed by the evangelists themselves. Thus, *every word in the gospels comes to us from the early Christians.*

This fact (and here I insist on the term *fact*) might not seem important all by itself. But it is absolutely crucial to bear it in mind because everything we have learned about the gospels in the last two centuries shows that the Christians who passed on the words and deeds of Jesus and the evangelists who wrote them down were anything but passive transmitters of what they received. On the contrary, they interpreted, explained, updated, embellished, and otherwise transformed what they passed on or wrote down. In this process, new material was developed and grafted onto what was already there. This means that a fundamental question that must be asked of every item in the gospels is: Does this look like something early Christians would have created in their effort to preach about their living Lord? If the initial answer is yes, the next question has to be whether there is any evidence that can help us trace it all the way back to Jesus himself. If not, a black vote may be the only option, not because we know for sure that this item entered the Christian tradition only after Easter, but because there is no evidence that it didn't.

It's not difficult to see how important all this is. It means that if a certain saying "sounds Christian" (and, obviously, a great deal in the gospels does), there is a presumption in favor of a black vote. A vote of any other color requires some countervailing evidence that, despite its Christian overtones, it goes back to the Jewish Jesus. Without such evidence, many (perhaps most) Fellows, myself included, were inclined to vote black.

Another reason for voting black is that a saying is judged to be what the Seminar calls "common lore," the kind of thing that everybody in a society knows and that anybody could say. Jesus surely said things like "good morning," "God bless you," and "what's for dinner?" He just as surely recited the commandments and said things like "Blessed be the Lord our God." But the only thing words like this reveal about Jesus is that he was like everyone else in his society. Many proverbs, folk sayings, and similar utterances by Jesus in the gospels were designated black (usually by consensus) not only because anyone could have said them, but also because even if Jesus did say them, they would tell us nothing distinctive about him. If Jesus' speech was not distinctive, it is impossible to understand why people would have bothered to remember and pass on what he said. Furthermore, if his speech was not distinctive, then by definition we have no chance of distinguishing it from that of other speakers of his day and thus no possibility of identifying the words of the historical Jesus. Hence, another meaning of a black designation is "Jesus may well have said this, but so could anyone else; it therefore tells us nothing distinctive about him."

EXCURSUS
Did Jesus Quote the Scriptures?

One group of sayings, most of which were voted black, deserve special attention because they are showcase examples of how the Seminar's conclusions can be rightly understood only if its methodological principles are taken into account. The sayings in question are those in which Jesus quotes some passage from the Hebrew Bible. A few of these sayings were voted black because they seem to be examples of common lore, such as Jesus' quotation of the commandment to honor parents (Mark 7:10). Most of them, however, were voted black because the early Christians used the Jewish scriptures to validate their belief that Jesus was the Messiah, the fulfillment of God's promises to Israel. It makes perfect sense that those Christians who passed on traditions about Jesus would have put the words of the scriptures onto his lips. This is especially the case for those sayings in which Jesus quotes the scriptures and then applies them to himself, thereby claiming that he was fulfilling a specific prophecy. So, unless there is some independent reason to think that biblical quotations attributed to Jesus actually reflected Jesus' own teaching (and in some cases there is),[3] these sayings are designated black.

Now here is where a misunderstanding can occur. Someone who didn't know about the principles behind the reasoning for black votes might infer from all the black ink that the Seminar denies that Jesus used the Hebrew Bible in his teaching. This would be a mistake. No Fellow believes that Jesus avoided quoting the scriptures. After all, Jesus was Jewish and discussing the scriptures, arguing over their interpretation, and applying them to various situations in life was a primary way for Jews of his day (and of all time) to talk about religion. All of us in the Seminar take it for granted that Jesus cherished the scriptures and made them the foundation for his own teaching. But this is also true of the Jews who spread the good news about Jesus and passed on his teaching after his death.

Thus, the Seminar's findings do not mean that the Seminar maintains that the historical Jesus didn't quote the Hebrew Bible. These findings indicate, rather, that because of the widespread use of the Jewish scriptures by the early Christians who preserved the traditions about Jesus, the Seminar could not make the case that the specific biblical quotations attributed to Jesus in the gospels originated with him rather than with his Christian followers.

Pink

Pink and gray results are inherently more complex than red or black ones because, while the latter necessarily emerge from consensus, the former might not. A pink designation can reflect widespread agreement that "Jesus probably said something like this." But it also can reflect a fairly broad spectrum of opinion among the Fellows. For example, the saying about the powerful man's house in Luke 11:21–22 is colored pink; the weighted average comes from a vote that was 24% red, 41% pink, 17% gray, and 17% black.* Because the colors are determined by averaging the votes, there are some

---

* At the theoretical extreme, a saying would be pink if its vote was 51% red and 49% black, but this situation never actually occurred. The most polarized vote for a pink saying was for the one about saving your life by losing it in Luke 17:33: 46% red, 0% pink, 18% gray, 36% black.

close calls. Four pink sayings would be red if only one or two Fellows had voted differently. Similarly, thirteen pink sayings would be gray if one or two Fellows had voted in the opposite direction.* Even with these qualifications, however, a pink designation still requires a sizeable majority of red and pink votes, or at least a near majority of red and pink votes with very few black ones. Thus, a pink designation for a saying usually means that a strong majority believed it certainly or probably comes from Jesus. But sometimes it means that there was a fair amount of uncertainty or divided opinion among the Fellows. At the very least it means that few were willing to vote it black. All told, there are seventy-five pink sayings on the final list.

Gray

Gray is the most difficult color to interpret and the Seminar debated its significance on several occasions. Like pink, gray represents the absence of a decisive collective judgment about a saying's historicity. Since the dividing lines between colors are based on statistical averages, there are many gray items that are nearly pink and some that are nearly black. But the problem is deeper than mathematics. The official definition of gray contains two independent clauses that pull in opposite directions: "Jesus did not say this, but the ideas contained in it are close to his own." The tension between these two halves of the definition raises a fundamental problem for interpreting the meaning of gray: is a gray vote a negative assessment of the historicity of a saying ("Jesus did not say this") or a positive one ("the ideas contained in it are close to his own")? Members of the Seminar are divided on this question.

My own position (and one shared by many Fellows) is that gray sayings are useful evidence for reconstructing the teaching of the historical Jesus, since they contain ideas that are close to his. (Keep in mind that many sayings printed in gray received a large number of pink votes, and even some red ones.)† Since this material is not red or pink, it must be used with nuance, but even nuanced evidence can be valuable. Other members of the Seminar maintain that gray material should seldom, if ever, be treated as evidence

---

* The pink saying closest to red is the parable of the Lost Coin in Luke 10:8–9, which received 45% red, 41% pink, 7% gray, 7% black. The pink saying closest to gray is the admonition "Don't turn away the one who tries to borrow from you" (Matt 5:42), for which the vote was 10% red, 35% pink, 52% gray, 3% black.

† Two good examples are the story about the rich man and Lazarus in Luke 16:19–26 (4% red, 46% pink, 21% gray, 29% black) and the admonition to pray in private in Matt 6:6a (8% red, 50% pink, 15% gray, 27% black).

about Jesus because using it like this unnecessarily injects an unacceptable level of speculation into the process.

A gray vote was also a way for Fellows to register their indecision. In the analysis of some sayings it seems clear that their literary settings in the gospels give them meanings that differ from the meanings they had in Jesus' own context. In some cases it is difficult to discern what that original meaning may have been. A few sayings are downright obscure in any context. Sometimes Fellows resorted to gray votes when they were convinced that a certain saying had not been created out of whole cloth by early Christians, but they could not decide what exactly Jesus would have meant by it. Sometimes indecision has nothing with do a saying's meaning, but simply with the ambiguities inherent in historical research. That is why there are many cases in which the same saying had some Fellows voting black and some voting red. Some members, myself included, sometimes voted gray when we could not decide what a saying meant. I often voted gray when I could not come to a clear decision, when good arguments were made both for red/pink and for black. In fact, one of the informal but official meanings finally adopted for gray is "Well, maybe." While some gray sayings reflect a consensus in the Seminar that they probably do not originate with Jesus, a good number of them point to various types of uncertainties among the Fellows.

Another reason that a large number of sayings are printed in gray is simply a lack of consensus within the Seminar. There are numerous sayings on which individual Fellows made decisive but divergent historical judgments. In these cases a gray coloring was not the result of a compromise vote, but rather the average of a sharply divided one. This is one reason why the Seminar not only prints the sayings in the gospels in four different colors, but also publishes the specific percentages of votes for each saying.[4]

The system of calculating weighted averages also makes for some statistical anomalies. For example, there are sayings printed in gray that received very few gray votes. The most striking example is the parable of The Sower in Luke 8:5–8, which received no gray votes at all (21% red, 43% pink, 0% gray, 36% black). Two other cases close to this extreme are the saying "As your Father" in Luke 6:36 (17% red, 42% pink, 8% gray, 33% black), and Thom 21:9 ("When the crop ripened, he came quickly carrying a sickle and harvested it": 11% red, 50% pink, 7% gray, 32% black). Also, it is good to remember that there are many gray sayings that some Fellows strongly believe should be black and probably just as many that others believe should be pink. The large "gray area" in the Seminar's findings leaves the door open for further investigation of these sayings.

Coloring the Deeds of Jesus

When the Seminar completed its works on the sayings of Jesus and took up the task of studying his deeds, we realized that the meanings assigned to the four colors had to be defined somewhat differently than they are for the sayings. The major reason for this is that there is an important difference between the way sayings and deeds are transmitted. The words attributed to Jesus in the gospels purport to be the sayings *of* Jesus, whereas the deeds attributed to him are stories *about* Jesus. Jesus' words can be *repeated*, but his deeds can only be *reported*.

If one of Jesus' sayings was remembered precisely as he said it and was passed on word for word, then those who hear it later experience the same saying as those who heard it from Jesus in person.* On the other hand, no matter how carefully the memories of Jesus' deeds were preserved, those who hear them recounted do not experience the same event as those who witnessed Jesus' deeds in person.

This difference between repeating and reporting is built into the historical process by the simple fact that the words and deeds of Jesus were passed on *in words*. Language is tailor made for transmitting words, but is an imperfect vehicle for preserving deeds. While it is sometimes possible to memorize and repeat exactly what you hear someone say (if it is very brief), you cannot replicate exactly what someone did by telling about it. Reports about events necessarily involve selectivity and interpretation. A report narrates only some of the numerous facets of the reality of an event, i.e., those the narrator was attending to and those he or she considers significant. Those who told stories about what Jesus had done had to shape their reports to a much greater extent than those who told about what Jesus had said.

Occasionally this shaping is so blatant that it is unmistakable. Two kinds of examples of this in the gospels are called narrator asides and narrative summaries. In an aside a narrator actually stops the story for a moment and speaks directly to the audience to supply some important information. Mark does this in his story about Jesus' family coming to take him away: Mark pauses to tell us, "You see, they thought he was out of his mind" (3:21). Occasionally a narrator aside will fill us in on something that not even an eyewitness would know, as when we are told what bystanders were thinking

---

* This is a theoretical ideal. In practice, nearly all the sayings of Jesus seem to have been paraphrased as they were passed on, though a few sayings could easily have been memorized exactly. Still, even a saying repeated word for word can take on a new meaning when told in a new context. Also, the process of translation, no matter how precise, can alter the meaning of a saying.

when they heard Jesus tell the paralytic that his sins were forgiven (Mark 2:6–7).

Narrative summaries are another obvious example of direct authorial intervention into the story. These brief passages do not narrate individual events, but rather summarize a whole series of them into a general report. A good example is Matt 9:35.

> And Jesus went about all the towns and villages, teaching in their synagogues and proclaiming the gospel of Heaven's imperial rule and healing every disease and ailment.

The consequences of all this for the Seminar's task is that while a saying's historicity must be assessed by analyzing the saying itself (that is, its very words), a report of a deed needs to be assessed, not in terms of the story itself, but in terms of the information contained within it. Put simply, the Seminar had to vote on a story's content, not on its wording. That is why the definitions of the colors for the deeds could not be borrowed directly from the definitions of the colors for the sayings. For example, the definition of a gray saying ("Jesus did not say this, but the ideas contained in it are close to his own") cannot be adapted in any straightforward way to apply to gray votes on a deed. After a number of different definitions were proposed and discussed, the Seminar settled on these:

Red The historical reliability of this information is virtually certain. It is supported by a preponderance of evidence.

Pink This information is probably reliable. It fits well with other evidence that is verifiable.

Gray This information is possible but unreliable. It lacks supporting evidence.

Black This information is improbable. It does not fit verifiable evidence; it is largely or entirely fictive.

As with the definitions for the sayings, these are not and cannot be precise. They leave a lot of room for judgment calls. For many Fellows, even after study and discussion, the choice between voting pink or gray or between gray or black on a given story was sometimes little more than playing a hunch. My own experience is probably representative of many other Fellows. Most of the time I had little trouble knowing what it meant to vote red or black. It was not always a simple task deciding whether the evidence and argument points to a verdict of "virtually certain" (red) or "largely or entirely fictive" (black), but at least the categories were readily intelligible. Things were not so clear when it came to voting pink or gray. What exactly is meant by "probably reliable" (pink) or "possible but unreliable" (gray)? And where is the boundary between them? (Statements like "I'm leaning toward a grayish pink vote" were often heard during discussions as we wrestled with some of the more historically ambiguous gospel stories.)

A rule of thumb I eventually came to rely on was to vote pink when I was fairly certain that the incident reported in the story had occurred but that its details had been invented in the process of passing it on. I often voted gray when I had significant doubts that the event had really occurred, but when I could also easily imagine it taking place, given what else I knew about Jesus and the historical context of his life. A good way to express informally what I meant by a gray vote is: "I don't think that this happened, but if some new evidence turned up that proved that it did, I wouldn't be surprised."

There is one more aspect of the Seminar's voting on the deeds that differs from its treatment of the sayings. In addition to voting on the specific stories in the gospels, the Seminar occasionally voted on historical statements that were derived from, but not actually contained in, the gospel stories. For example, besides voting on the individual passages that report Jesus eating with tax collectors, prostitutes, and other sinners, the Seminar voted (red) that "Jesus openly consorted with social outcasts."

We arrived at this procedure out of a desire to distill specific items of significant historical information from the various stories. This is another way to cope with the fact that all the historical information in the gospels comes to us embedded in stories. The evangelists and those before them who passed on the information about what Jesus had done expressed all of it in stories (mostly in anecdotes); they did not pass it on as lists of facts. As a result there are a good number of scenes in the gospels that look like typifications, stories about the kind of things Jesus was known for. When those stories are analyzed one by one, they may bear so many traces of having been shaped by the oral tradition or of having been composed by the evangelist that these stories, considered individually, do not pass historical muster. And yet when similar stories are taken as a group, they may collectively point to an authentic memory about the way Jesus acted.

A star example has to do with the exorcism stories. The gospels contain six individual stories of Jesus casting out evil spirits,[5] as well as narrative reports and summaries such as we find in Matt 8:16 (. . . "they brought many who were demon-possessed to him. He drove out the spirits with a command" . . .). Of these six stories, five were voted gray and one black. Yet the memory of Jesus the exorcist is so firmly rooted in the tradition that the Seminar believed that the gray results give only part of the historical picture. So we discussed and voted red on the statement: "Jesus drove out what were thought to be demons." This conveys our judgment that it is historically certain that Jesus' contemporaries believed him to be an exorcist, but that we doubt that any of the individual exorcisms in the gospels relate specific historical events. In other words, the Seminar believes that, based on the solid fact that Jesus was remembered as an exorcist, the evangelists and others made up individual stories of Jesus releasing people from the grip of evil spirits.

Having all the sayings and deeds of Jesus sorted into four colors is a uniquely useful resource for those interested in studying the historical Jesus and the historicity of the gospels. The color of a passage is a rough indicator of its relative degree of historical reliability. The definitions of the four colors are necessarily broad and the distinctions between red and pink, between pink and gray, and between gray and black are necessarily imprecise. But it is no defect that the colors are approximations. That is all they can be, for three reasons. 1) The nature of the material in the gospels seldom lends itself to precise historical judgments. 2) The colors represent the end result of a collaborative process that takes into account the individual judgments of all the members of the Seminar. Sometimes the Fellows achieved consensus in their findings; sometimes their individual conclusions were widely diverse. 3) Each color represents a fairly wide range of statistical results generated by the Seminar's use of the mathematical device of weighted averages. There can thus be a significant difference between items of the same color that fall on opposite ends of the range assigned to that color.

All of this shows that if you want to use the Seminar's findings to full advantage, you should take into account the actual voting results, ragged though they sometimes are, and not simply take the printed colors at face value.

The Reasoning Behind the Votes

In addition to the quandaries about the meaning of the colors, there is another problem that can complicate understanding the results of the Seminar: the limitations on comprehending the rationale for the Fellows' votes. There are three aspects of this problem.

1. The first limitation is imposed by the sheer amount of material treated in *The Five Gospels* and *The Acts of Jesus*. These books report the Seminar's analysis of all the individual sayings and stories in the Gospels of Mark, Matthew, Luke, John, Thomas, and Peter. Each book weighs in at over 550 pages. Their comprehensive scope made it necessary to condense the explanations for the votes on individual items. Because of this constraint, the comments focus on what is most important: outlining the major reasons for

the color in which each saying and story is printed. This is fine for items on which there was a consensus in the Seminar, but for items whose color represents an average of diverse votes, there is simply not enough space to explain minority opinions in detail. For example, the chapter on Luke in *The Five Gospels* is 130 pages long, with over a third of that space taken up by the text of the gospel itself. The Seminar cast over 380 votes on the sayings in Luke,* which gives you some idea why the explanations can only be generalized summaries. Unless these books were to run to thousands of pages, the explanations had to pass over interesting nuances in the Seminar's deliberations. The advantage of *The Five Gospels* and *The Acts of Jesus* is that they report in two volumes the full range of the Seminar's work and make available a brief analysis of every saying and story in the six relevant gospels. They achieve their purpose well and cannot be faulted for not doing the impossible.

2. The second aspect of the limits to understanding the rationale for votes is more fundamental than the limits imposed by the practicalities of publishing. Even if there were unlimited space for explaining the votes, a full accounting would still elude us. This is because the Jesus Seminar is a collective body, not an individual.

To appreciate the problem this entails, it may help to consider an analogous case, the U.S. Congress. When Congress votes we know the result and we can easily discover how each member voted, but the reasons for the votes differ from member to member. "Congress voted to cut taxes" reports a simple fact, but "Congress lowered taxes because it feared a recession" is an over-simplified generalization. Not every member who voted to lower taxes did so for that reason. Those who did may have had other motives as well. Besides, the generalization ignores completely the members who voted in the minority. With the Jesus Seminar the situation is even more complicated than with Congress: members of Congress can only vote yes or no, whereas members of the Seminar can vote in four different ways. Hence, statements like "the Seminar believes X" or "the Fellows are of the opinion Y" need to be understood for the generalizations they are. Some critics of the Seminar (who ought to know better) and some media reporters (who have no excuse at all) have ignored this and have conveyed the erroneous impression that there is little diversity of opinion among members of the Seminar.

---

* Separate votes were often taken on different parts of the same item, especially in the case of sayings that contain redactional additions.

Another thing to keep in mind is that different Fellows attend different meetings. No two meetings have had identical participant rosters. This raises the question whether certain items would have received a different spread of votes if a different mix of members had been present. On a few occasions I suspected, especially in the cases of very close votes, that a specific saying or deed might have ended up with a different color if it had been on the agenda of another meeting.

3. A final factor complicating a full understanding of the work of the Seminar is that its protocols make it all but impossible to discover the rationale for each member's vote. Fellows do their work with complete intellectual freedom. They reach conclusions as individuals, judging the evidence by whatever standards they believe most appropriate. All voting is done privately, either by secret ballot or by dropping beads in such a way that no one knows how anyone else votes. During discussion some Fellows declare how they intend to vote, in their attempts to persuade others to join them, but Fellows are not accountable for their votes. They are under no obligation to explain why they voted a certain way or even to announce how they voted.

All this makes it challenging to give an accurate account of why members voted the way they did on certain items. Fellows who prepare the reports from each meeting and the author-editors who contribute to the Seminar's official publications study the position papers and whatever notes of the discussion are available. They can consult the video tapes made of every session of the Seminar. Even so, the secrecy of the voting leaves gaps in understanding the reasons for the specific spread of votes on some items. Having done a fair amount of this type of analysis myself, I must admit that sometimes I just had to make my best guess. For a number of sayings, after I reviewed the papers and my notes, I could not remember even how I had voted.

It is seldom a simple matter to understand why a saying is colored the way it is. The various interpretations of the colors, the system of weighted averages, and the secrecy of the vote can all add layers of complexity to the situation. This means that you cannot learn a great deal about a saying merely by knowing its color. If, for example, a saying is pink, you know that the verdict of the Seminar is that Jesus probably said something like this. As a generalized statement, this is true. However, a critical reader needs also to be aware that not all the Fellows (perhaps not even a majority of them) voted pink; that those who did vote pink may have had a variety of reasons for doing so; that those who voted other colors had intelligent reasons for their votes; that at a different meeting the vote might have gone differently; that the explanatory comments in *The Five Gospels* and *The Acts of Jesus* of necessity skip a lot of detail and nuance; and that only God knows the full reasons for every member's vote.

Readers will respond in different ways when they dwell on all this complexity. Their responses will depend largely on what they are looking for in *The Five Gospels* and *The Acts of Jesus*. If they are hoping for a guaranteed list of things Jesus really said and did and things he really didn't say and do, they will be disappointed. No doubt there are some looking for books with all the answers, for written authorities that relieve them of the responsibility to do their own thinking and form their own judgments. Such readers will either be disappointed that *The Five Gospels* and *The Acts of Jesus* do not meet their expectations, or they will use these books simplistically, and end up misleading themselves and misrepresenting the Seminar. On the other hand, those who seek an alternative to uncritical literalism or authoritarian fundamentalism and who welcome intellectually demanding reading that can inform their own thinking and empower their own search for the historical Jesus can use *The Five Gospels* and *The Acts of Jesus* with great profit.

The best way to regard the work of the Jesus Seminar is to see it as opening a door and pointing the way. The Seminar opens the door to a formerly closed room and it points to a new way of understanding Jesus. We are proud of this landmark accomplishment and we hope it is received as a valuable service. But it is only a first step. Our readers must enter that room on their own and must set out on that way for themselves. It would be a disservice to the Seminar and a distortion of its work if its decisions were taken as the last word on the matter. The scholars of the Seminar hope that their work will invite and enable others to join them on the search for the historical Jesus. It would be a disappointing irony if our judgments were "taken as gospel."

Part Two

Part Two deals with the controversy among scholars over the work of the Jesus Seminar and, more generally, over the historical-critical approach to the Bible.

Chapter 4, "The Jesus Seminar and its Critics," responds to criticisms of the Seminar that followed in the wake of the publication of *The Five Gospels*. The popularity of this book with the public and the unusual amount of media attention the Seminar received because of it provoked a barrage of criticism from scholars defending the orthodoxies of the church and the academy. In this chapter I discuss criticisms regarding the Seminar's practice of voting, the composition of its membership, its assessment of the Gospel of Thomas, and its finding that Jesus was not an apocalypticist. I also examine the curious charge that the Seminar's historical Jesus is not Jewish. I close by offering a moral assessment of the ugly language in which some scholars denounce the Seminar.

Chapters 5, 6, and 7 are detailed engagements with two important critics of the Seminar, Luke Timothy Johnson and Ben Witherington. Both of these scholars attack not only the work of the Jesus Seminar, but the very project of reconstructing the historical Jesus out of critical assessments of the gospels. Instead they derive portraits of Jesus from the christological perspectives of the canonical gospels. That is, Johnson and Witherington both believe that legitimate biblical scholarship leads us to the risen Christ professed by traditional Christianity rather than the historical Jesus reconstructed by critical scholars. However, Johnson and Witherington maintain this position for very different, even opposite, reasons. Johnson does so because he is radically skeptical about the historicity of the gospels. According to Johnson the historical Jesus is irretrievably lost to us. Johnson argues that biblical scholarship should focus on the canonical Jesus (the christological portraits of Jesus in the canonical gospels) because that is all we have: virtually nothing in the gospels is historically reliable. For Witherington on the other hand, the historical Jesus *is* the canonical Jesus because virtually everything in the gospels is historically reliable. Though Witherington is not a literalist in any simplistic sense, he maintains that all the gospel material, from beginning to end, is solidly anchored in accurate historical memories about Jesus. As he sees it, the canonical gospels present

Jesus the way he presented himself. For Witherington then, reconstructing the historical Jesus does not entail sifting the gospel evidence to ascertain which parts are historically accurate and which are not. Rather, it entails fitting all the gospel material into a composite portrait of a figure who was both historical and divine.

Chapter 5, "History is Not Optional," is a critique of Johnson's *The Real Jesus*, a broadside attack on historical Jesus research that Johnson says he wrote because of his alarm at the Jesus Seminar. I analyze Johnson's harsh denunciations of other scholars and respond to his criticisms of recent studies on Jesus. I probe the roots and implications of Johnson's extreme skepticism about the historical value of the gospels. Finally, I examine Johnson's argument that the existence of early Christianity cannot be explained historically, but can only be attributed to the divine miracle of Jesus' resurrection.

Chapter 6, "The Jesus of Orthodoxy and the Jesuses of the Gospels," continues my critique of Johnson's *The Real Jesus* from another angle. Johnson maintains that the gospels do not yield reliable historical knowledge about Jesus' life or teachings. He argues instead that they can mediate to us a reliable understanding of the risen Lord of Christian experience because they all present the religious meaning of Jesus' life according to a single pattern. I compare the pattern Johnson claims to find against the evidence in the gospels and argue that no such single pattern exists, and thus that the gospels do not support the theological orthodoxy to which Johnson wants to subordinate biblical scholarship.

Chapter 7, "Can the Historical Jesus Be Made Safe for Othodoxy?", is a critique of Witherington's *The Jesus Quest*. After responding to some of his criticisms of the Jesus Seminar, I examine his curious position that the historical Jesus was a non-committal apocalypticist: one who preached that the End *might* be near. Next I criticize Witherington's argument that the historical Jesus understood himself to be a divine being, Wisdom Incarnate. Finally, I speculate about the kind of audience that would find Witherington's scholarship persuasive.

Chapter 8, "Christian Apologetics and the Resurrection," is an adaptation of my contribution to a debate about the historicity of the resurrection stories, a debate that involved three members of the Jesus Seminar and three of its evangelical critics. While this chapter is not a direct reply to criticisms of the Seminar, I have included it in this book because it shows how the principles of historical investigation used by the Seminar lead to different results than do the principles used by scholars who defend the historical accuracy of the gospels.

After explaining what Christian apologetics is, I discuss why apologies do not persuade those who do not already believe what the apologies are defending. I propose that the real function of apologetics is to reassure insiders rather than persuade outsiders, which, I argue, is also true of the gospels. I then apply this to the resurrection by analyzing the peculiar story in Matthew's gospel about the righteous Jews who rose from the dead when Jesus died. I maintain that Matthew knew this story was historical fiction and expected his audience to take it symbolically, not literally. I then argue that, for all we can tell, Matthew understood his story about the resurrection of Jesus in the same way. Finally, I conclude that the resurrection stories are like apologies in that they were not intended to convince outsiders, but to strengthen the faith of those who already believed in the resurrection.

CHAPTER FOUR

The Jesus Seminar
and its Critics

The Jesus Seminar has received a good deal of attention from scholars, most of it negative. In this chapter I will identify key areas of disagreement between the Seminar and its critics. It is not my primary aim here to respond to them, though I will do so on a few points. Rather, I hope to clarify the issues in two ways. First, I will identify a few items on which critics misunderstand the Seminar and try to clear things up. Second, I will examine the assumptions implicit in their criticisms and gauge the extent of substantive agreement and disagreement between the Seminar and its critics.

A number of critiques of the Seminar have appeared in print. In this chapter I focus on the criticisms of five respected scholars: Richard Hays,[1] Luke Johnson,[2] Howard Kee,[3] Birger Pearson,[4] and Ben Witherington.[5] Their criticisms are representative of the rest and fully sufficient for my purpose.

My analysis will cluster around five topics raised by these critics: the Seminar's practice of voting and its willingness to address the public; whether the Seminar reflects a consensus among biblical scholars; its work on the Gospel of Thomas; its conclusion that Jesus was not an apocalypticist; and whether the Seminar's Jesus is sufficiently Jewish. I will close this chapter with a brief remark on the unusually intense polemical language used by the Seminar's critics.

VOTING AND THE PUBLIC

Some critics take a dim view of the Seminar's practice of voting on the authenticity of the sayings and deeds attributed to Jesus. For example, Ben Witherington complains that only in a country where majority views are assumed to be right and where "truth" is decided by voting could this idea of voting on Jesus have arisen.[6] However, as *The Five Gospels* explains, the Jesus Seminar got the idea, not from American democracy, but from the practice of various biblical translation committees and from the

Sections of this chapter originally appeared in "The Jesus Seminar and its Critics: What is Really at Stake?, *The Fourth R* 10.1/2 (January–February 1997), pp. 17–27.

United Bible Society committees that vote on the critical edition of the Greek text of the New Testament.[7]

Luke Johnson has no objection to translation committees voting because "these votes are carried out privately."[8] Johnson's remark is revealing: it shows that for him the real offense of the Jesus Seminar is not that it votes, but that it does its work in public. Numerous snide comments about the Seminar being hungry for publicity show that other critics also resent the public face of the Seminar.

In an attempt to estimate the depth of this resentment, let me pose a hypothetical scenario. What if the same people in the Jesus Seminar had carried out the same project and had come up with the same results, but had done so in a Society of Biblical Literature seminar and published the results in *Semeia*, the Society's journal for experimental scholarship? Certainly the public would not have paid any attention, but my question is: how much attention would this project have received from *scholars*? I suspect, but obviously cannot prove, that the quantity of the critical response would be much less and its quality much better. I suspect also that the sheer nastiness of the insulting rhetoric directed against the Seminar would be much reduced.

The acerbic response of the Seminar's critics to its commitment to work in public seems to rest on the assumption that academics who speak publicly about religion should keep their views to themselves if they might be unsettling to the beliefs of mainstream Christians. (This assumption explains why biblical scholars have largely left it up to scientists to battle creationism in the public forum.) The fact that journalists who cover religion could register such shock when scholars use words like "non-historical" (or, worse yet, " fiction") to characterize some gospel passages shows what a good job biblical scholars have done keeping their secrets to themselves.

CONSENSUS

Nearly all critics of the Jesus Seminar object, some of them strenuously, to the notion that the Seminar's views reflect a consensus among New Testament scholars. Two quotations can illustrate the gist of this criticism. Richard Hays states that the Seminar's "attempt to present their views as 'the assured results of critical scholarship' is—one must say it—reprehensible deception."[9] Similarly, Howard Kee states, "The Seminar's claim to speak for the majority of scholars is grossly inaccurate."[10]

The most important thing to say in response to this criticism is that it is almost certainly wrong. It is highly doubtful that the Seminar actually claims to speak for a scholarly consensus. I say "almost certainly" and "doubtful" simply because one can never prove a negative. However, I have looked carefully for such claims in *The Five Gospels* and *The Acts of Jesus* and have not found any. Perhaps others have, but I have not located a single quotation in anything published in the Seminar's name that makes this sweeping claim, nor have the critics to whom I wrote asking for the page numbers on which these claims can be found.[11]

In some places the Seminar expresses positions that it claims are those held by most New Testament scholars. So let me express my understanding of what the Seminar actually means by this claim, in the solid confidence that my understanding is shared by everyone I know in the Seminar. I have never understood our claim to speak for scholars to mean that most scholars agree with our specific findings or even with all of our methods. (Not even members of the Seminar agree on these.) What I do understand it to mean is that the Seminar's fundamental views about the gospels—that some of the words attributed to Jesus were not actually spoken by him; that the gospels contain historical memory from before Calvary and religious interpretation from after it; that they are, to put it bluntly, a complex blend of fact and fiction; and that to discover the historical Jesus we need a critical sifting of evidence rather than theological assurances—that these views *do* represent the consensus among critical scholars.

While this is not news to scholars, *it is news to the American public*. A huge number of Americans believe that inerrancy is the only legitimate approach to the Bible, that to take the Bible seriously is to take it literally. Critics are right to protest that many scholars disagree with the Seminar's results, but they do a disservice if they perpetuate the impression that doubts about the historical accuracy of significant portions of the gospels are confined to some radical splinter group. This is important because critics assert that the Jesus Seminar is little more than a "faction" with "idiosyncratic opinions." I wish that reporters who interview critics of the Seminar would ask *them* which items in the gospels *they* consider non-historical. If critics were to answer this question honestly, it would signal that the Seminar's views on the general nature of the gospels are shared by virtually all critical scholars, even though many of them disagree with the Seminar's specific results.

Several critics point out that members of the Jesus Seminar are "self-selected" and they clearly intend this to be a criticism. But this is puzzling. Self-selection can only be a criticism on the assumption that membership in this kind of group should not be by self-selection. How then? By invitation only? The Jesus Seminar is open to anyone with the proper academic credentials. It has no way to exclude anyone who is qualified who wants to join.

What if membership was by invitation only? Would that make the Seminar more credible? And if members were not self-selected, who should do the selecting? Criticizing the Seminar because it is self-selected amounts to criticizing it for not being elitist.[12]

Critics also argue that the Seminar's composition is such that its members are not a representative sample of mainstream scholars. For example, Luke Johnson asserts that members of the Jesus Seminar "by no means represent the cream of New Testament scholarship in this country . . . Most of the participants are in relatively undistinguished academic positions."[13]

Well, wait just a minute. Since I don't wish to embarrass anyone, I will use myself as an example. I am not in a "relatively undistinguished academic position." I am in an *absolutely* undistinguished one. I teach at a college that is so obscure I've yet to meet anyone at Society of Biblical Literature meetings who's heard of it. I teach four courses per semester. My college does not grant sabbaticals. I have very little time for scholarly work. I am, in short, an academic working stiff—which makes me like most biblical scholars in this country. I am much more representative of the rank and file of the Society of Biblical Literature than those in distinguished positions on the graduate faculties at elite universities. Richard Hays goes so far as to list the prestigious graduate institutions without members of the Seminar on the faculty: Yale, Harvard, Princeton, Duke, the University of Chicago, Union Theological Seminary, Vanderbilt, Southern Methodist University, and Catholic University.[14] Luke Johnson's article shows some literary dependence on Hays', but when it comes to the list of distinguished institutions Johnson redacts Hays' roster to include Emory University, where Johnson teaches.[15]

The various criticisms about consensus raise an underlying question: how do we know what the scholarly consensus is on a given issue? Richard Hays states, "Let it be said clearly—most professional biblical scholars are profoundly skeptical of the methods and conclusions of this academic splinter group."[16] How does Hays know this to be true? How do we determine when there is a consensus? I am willing to bet that there are consensus positions among New Testament scholars on a few basic issues, such as the existence of Q, the priority of Mark, and the pseudonymity of the Pastoral Epistles. But if this claim were challenged, how would I demonstrate it? The standard method in scholarly writing is to fill our footnotes with references pro and con on a given position. But this counts only published opinions. It would be fascinating for the Society of Biblical Literature to poll its members on a broad range of basic questions. That would give us some hard data from which to assess where the consensus positions are. But even this would have weaknesses. Biblical scholarship is highly specialized and so a scholar's position on an issue outside his or her area of specialization may not be all that informed. (For example, some scholars who make confident claims about the Gospel of Thomas cannot read Coptic, the language in which the only extant copy of this gospel is preserved.) Many of the opinions of biblical scholars are simply not expert opinions. So should we give credence only to the consensus among experts? If so, who decides who is on the list of experts? I suggest that in the absence of reliable statistical data we really don't know enough to state with any assurance at all what the consensus views are on most issues. (When the Jesus Seminar reports a consensus among its members, it provides exact figures that allow one to measure its extent.)

Another question raised by the squabbling over scholarly consensus is: why is it so important for us to claim that consensus is on our side? It's not too difficult to figure this out. We believe that scholarly consensus confers authority. And authority confers power, the kind of power we scholars crave, the power of persuasion. Especially when we address the public, or our students, to say that position X is the position of the vast majority of scholars is a power play. It says: if you don't agree with it, you're either uninformed or you're not very smart. There is nothing wrong, per se, with power plays. But we owe it to ourselves and to our audiences, especially to our students, to be circumspect about how we use them.

THE GOSPEL OF THOMAS

One distinctive aspect of the Jesus Seminar's work is its commitment to investigating all early Christian sources regardless of their canonical status. In its work on the sayings of Jesus, the Seminar gave careful attention to one gospel outside the New Testament, the Gospel of Thomas. The title of the Seminar's publication, *The Five Gospels*, indicates how important the Seminar believes this gospel to be for understanding the historical Jesus. Virtually all the Seminar's critics discuss its treatment of Thomas.

In introducing this gospel to readers, critics of the Seminar emphasize its gnostic character. Howard Kee states that "the *whole* of the Gospel of Thomas" is a "radical Gnostic reworking of the Jesus tradition."[17] Birger Pearson asserts that Thomas is "*completely* dominated by a (probably Syrian) type of Christianity oriented to mysticism and informed by the myth of the descent and ascent of the soul."[18] Such characterizations are surely over-stated. Many sayings in Thomas have no gnostic or mystical content at all. Some of them are close parallels to their canonical counterparts.

Everyone grants that Thomas has its own distinctive theological tenden-cies and that it has reworked a lot (but not all) of its material accordingly. But how does that make Thomas different from any other gospel? Isn't Matthew a thorough reworking of Mark? Isn't John's reworking of the Jesus tradition just as radical as that of Thomas'? Critics of the Seminar apparently assume that Thomas' gnosticizing interpretation is so pervasive that earlier, non-gnostic, material cannot be distinguished. In fact, the redactional mod-ifications that reflect a gnostic perspective are usually utterly obvious, almost hamfisted, and are easily detachable from earlier material.

Within the Seminar there is consensus that Thomas is not dependent on the canonical gospels. Critics rightly note that this question is not settled among scholars in general. However, most critics agree with the Seminar that Thomas contains sayings that are early and independent. This is very important, for it means that both the Seminar and nearly all its critics agree that Thomas cannot be left out of historical Jesus research.[19]

Birger Pearson's analysis of the Seminar's use of Thomas is puzzling. He charges that the Seminar's assumptions about Thomas are "quite naive,"[20] but then observes that of all the sayings unique to Thomas, the Seminar found only two that it could plausibly trace to Jesus. Pearson agrees with these results and so, presumably, does not consider them naive. This is puz-zling because one expects naive assumptions to produce naive results. The implication, then, is that the Seminar's methods must have corrected for the alleged naiveté of its assumptions. This is high praise indeed, though I doubt that Pearson intended it.

An assumption about Thomas that I brought with me to the Seminar was that Thomas would shed new light on the historical Jesus. This assumption proved to be unfounded. Of the sayings unique to Thomas, the Seminar voted none red and only two pink. Judging from the Seminar's results, Thomas tells us almost nothing about Jesus that we didn't already know from the other gospels. Nevertheless, the Seminar's findings on Thomas show that this gospel makes a valuable contribution to our understanding of Jesus. This aspect of the Seminar's work has not been noted by critics and so I want to draw attention to it here. If the Seminar is right in its assessment that Thomas is an independent source, then Thomas provides multiple indepen-dent attestation for a number of otherwise singly-attested canonical sayings. By my count, there are thirty-two such items. This means that the Jesus Seminar's use of Thomas has the result of *increasing* our confidence in the historical reliability of a good deal of canonical material. This needs to be appreciated because a few critics (like Johnson) assume that the Seminar's attention to Thomas challenges the authority of the canon. The actual work of the Seminar shows such an assumption to be a caricature.

One detail noted by most critics is the reference in *The Five Gospels* to an early "first edition" of Thomas. They object that there is no evidence for such a document. Here the critics are right. The Seminar concludes that some sayings in Thomas are as early as their parallels in Mark and Q, and that a few may be even earlier. Thus the earliest layer of tradition in Thomas is as early as the earliest layer of the synoptic tradition. But the first time I saw or heard a reference to an early first edition of Thomas was in the Seminar's own publications. To set the record straight as best I can, few members of the Seminar subscribe to this theory and I consider it unfortunate that this new and controversial theory is put forth as if it were an established position. However, the substance of the claim that there was an early first edition is that Thomas contains material as early as the synoptics, something on which the Seminar and its critics essentially agree.

APOCALYPTIC

For the public the most controversial aspect of the Jesus Seminar is that it does not accept the literal historicity of each verse in the gospels. But for scholars the most controversial aspect of the Seminar is that its historical Jesus is not an apocalyptic figure. Of all the Seminar's findings, this is the one is that its critics contest most vigorously.

Critics charge that the Seminar assumed a priori that Jesus was not an apocalypticist and then classified apocalyptic material in the gospels as inauthentic on the basis of that assumption. Such a charge accuses the Seminar of dishonesty. For example, Howard Kee refers to the Seminar's "manipulation of evidence in order to rid Jesus of an apocalyptic outlook," a procedure he calls "prejudgment masquerading as scholarship."[21] Richard Hays asserts, the "Jesus Seminar employs its conviction that Jesus was a non-eschatological thinker as a stringent criterion for sorting the authenticity of the sayings material" and, "an a priori construal of Jesus and his message governs the critical judgment made about individual sayings."[22] Luke Johnson charges that Jesus' eschatology is "simply dismissed without significant argument."[23]

From my perspective as a member of the Seminar, it is clear that this is a major misunderstanding of what really happened in the Seminar.[24] I believe this misunderstanding results from two factors. The first is that, although *The Five Gospels* never actually says that apocalyptic sayings were assumed to be inauthentic, it does in some places give this impression. This is unfortunate because it is misleading. The second factor is the willingness of some critics of the Seminar to assume that its members lack intellectual integrity.

Since there is a good deal of misunderstanding about how the Seminar arrived at its conclusion on this matter, it may help if I relate my own experience. I joined the Seminar one year after I received my Ph.D. I had not specialized in historical Jesus studies as a graduate student. To be honest, I had not thought very deeply about whether Jesus was an apocalyptic prophet. I assumed that he had been one because I had absorbed the traditional wisdom of New Testament scholarship. In preparing for Seminar meetings over several years, I worked through all the apocalyptic sayings one by one. Though I was predisposed to consider this kind of material authentic, I was persuaded time and again by both the position papers and the debates to vote gray or black. Some learned and respected members argued in favor of the apocalyptic Jesus but the votes consistently went against them. (Unfortunately, most of the members who championed the apocalyptic Jesus eventually left the Seminar.) Some members had studied the issue extensively and had moved away from the apocalyptic portrait of Jesus before the Seminar had been formed. However, my impression is that most of us were like me: without strong positions either way and open to being persuaded by the evidence in the texts and the arguments of other scholars. I do not mean to imply that everyone who studies the material the way I did will reach the same conclusions. I am only saying that this is how it happened for me. I have no writings on this topic to defend and no scholarly reputation to uphold. This, plus my undistinguished academic position, testify that I have no professional stake in this matter. (There is a certain freedom in being marginal.)

For critics of the Seminar, the apocalypticism of Jesus is so self-evident that it functions not simply as a foundational premise, but as something even more basic, virtually as an axiom. For example, Ben Witherington states that the Seminar "omitted, almost entirely, the theological and eschatological matrix out of which *all* Jesus' teaching operates."[25] Birger Pearson asserts that a non-apocalyptic Jesus "is not only intrinsically improbable but strains credulity to its breaking point."[26] Pearson makes the intriguing claim that even the sayings that the Seminar colored red and pink are shot through with apocalyptic eschatology. Pearson concludes that Seminar members were not intelligent enough to notice this. Pearson turns the words of Luke 17:21 against the Seminar: "I would submit that eschatology is present 'right there in (the scholars') presence', but they 'don't see it'."[27] He also refers to "the Seminar's failure to notice the eschatology in their data base."[28]

A conclusion at least as plausible as Pearson's is that, despite the Seminar's alleged ideologically-driven effort to root out apocalyptic from the historical Jesus, its criteria and methods were so sound that they led the Seminar to results contrary to its ideology. However, a more realistic possiblity is that, contrary to Pearson, these red and pink sayings need not be read apocalyptically. A number of these sayings acquire their apocalyptic coloring from their literary contexts, or from interpretive comments that are very probably secondary, or from the apocalyptic framework within which scholars place them. However, if considered on their own terms apart from their literary contexts, secondary interpretations, and exegetical frameworks, their apocalyptic character is far from obvious and, in some cases, simply not there. Showcase examples are the parables of The Sower and The Mustard Seed. Other examples are Luke 17:33 ("Whoever tries to save his life will lose it, but whoever loses his life will save it") and the beatitudes on those who are hungry and those who weep (Luke 6:20). The question here is whether every reference to a future state of affairs is necessarily eschatological.

Birger Pearson goes so far as to argue that even sayings that explicitly proclaim the presence of the kingdom are eschatological, not because of what they say, but because of the context within which he insists they should be interpreted. According to Pearson, Luke 11:20 is apocalyptic (despite its announcement that the kingdom "has arrived") because it deals with exorcism. For Pearson even Luke 17:20–21 ("God's rule is right there in your presence") is apocalyptic: Pearson asserts that "the key to its proper interpretation" is Luke 11:20.[29]

Pearson's analysis of The Empty Jar and The Assassin, the two authentic parables that are unique to the Gospel of Thomas, is even more specious. He maintains that these must be understood eschatologically, not because of what they say, but because they need to be read the same way as other parables that Pearson takes to be eschatological. He argues that the parable of The Empty Jar (Thomas 97) "can be compared" to the parable of The Wise and Foolish Maidens (Matt 25:1–12) and that the parable of The Assassin (Thomas 98) should be read in the context of The Tower Builder (Luke 14:28–30) and The Warring King (Luke 14:31–32). He holds that "once the eschatology is removed" from these two Thomas parables, they "are reduced to pure nonsense."[30] Pearson's objection to "removing" these parables' eschatology begs the question because there is no eschatology to "remove." The eschatology Pearson sees in them is imported from the context he creates. Thomas 97 and 98 appear eschatological only if one reads into them the eschatology of the other parables Pearson selects (and the eschatology of The Tower Builder and The Warring King is far from obvious).

I believe this whole question is an open one. The presence and extent of apocalyptic in Jesus' sayings is an issue over which scholars can have a fair fight. Here I only want to point out the arbitrariness of the assumption that if a saying *can* be read apocalyptically, then it *must* be read that way.

Another recurrent criticism of the Jesus Seminar is that its non-apocalyptic Jesus would not have gotten crucified. The assumption here is that an apocalyptic message (which may or may not include explicit or implicit messianic claims) is both the necessary and sufficient cause for Jesus' execution. But this assumption does not hold up under scrutiny. An apocalyptic message by itself did not get you killed. If it did, the entire Qumran community would have been snuffed out in a mass execution. An apocalyptic message has to combined with something else for its messenger to become a political threat. But this is as true for a non-apocalyptic message. Wouldn't anyone who disrupted the temple during Passover season on the scale that Jesus is reported to have done be perceived as a dangerous troublemaker, regardless of his message, or even if he had no particular message at all?

A (NON-)JEWISH JESUS

The most acerbic criticism of the Seminar is that its Jesus is not Jewish. Two examples illustrate the contempt with which this criticism is made. Richard Hays charges that the Seminar's portrait of Jesus is

an ahistorical fiction achieved by the surgical removal of Jesus from his Jewish context. The fabrication of a non-Jewish Jesus is one particularly pernicious side effect of the Jesus Seminar's methodology.[31]

Birger Pearson takes Hays surgical imagery to prurient proportions:

The Jesus of the Jesus Seminar is a non-Jewish Jesus. To put it metaphorically, the Seminar has performed a forcible epispasm on the historical Jesus, a surgical procedure removing the marks of his circumcision.[32]

The tone in which critics make this accusation is unmistakably derogatory, but what exactly does it mean that the Seminar's Jesus is not Jewish? The historical Jesus that emerges from the work of the Jesus Seminar is the implied author/speaker of the ninety sayings that the Seminar judged authentic (red and pink in the Seminar's color code). Therefore, to claim that this Jesus is not Jewish can only mean that the implied speaker of The Good Samaritan and The Prodigal Son, the one who invoked God as *abba* and pronounced blessings on the poor, and so on—that whoever said these things was not Jewish. I doubt that critics really intend this judgment, but if they do not, then the accusation that the Seminar's Jesus is not Jewish lacks specific content and so should be regarded as vacuous rhetoric.[33]

Stepping back from the rhetorical heat of this accusation, we can tease out an assumption on which it stands. This assumption is that we know enough about Galilean Judaism in the first third of the first century to be able to recognize what could and could not have been part of it. Does anyone really want to own that assumption? If not, the criticism evaporates because there are no secure grounds on which it could be either substantiated or rebutted.

The Jewishness of Jesus is a phony issue. The accusation that the Jesus Seminar strips Jesus of his Judaism is a powerful attention-getter.[34] But it is an accusation without specific content. Everyone in the historical Jesus debate agrees that Jesus was Jewish. The real question is what kind of Jew he was.

Accusing the Seminar of negating Jesus' Jewishness is a red herring, but it carries an assumption that is worth exploring. This is the assumption that identity is constituted by markers of distinctiveness. Only on this assumption could one reason that if a given reconstruction of the historical Jesus does not make topics like covenant, law, messiah, and apocalyptic central to Jesus' teaching then that Jesus is not Jewish. This is rather like saying that I must not be Catholic if I don't put the Pope or the Virgin Mary at the center of my religious language. This way of framing the issue of religious identity opens a back door into the thorny issue of the criterion of dissimilarity. The Seminar ran aground on this issue repeatedly and vigorously debated it on numerous occasions. Eventually most of us seem to have settled on a soft version of dissimilarity that Robert Funk calls "distinctiveness." If Jesus' speech was not distinctive in his own Jewish context, then why did people bother to remember it and pass it on? If it is not distinctive vis-a-vis later Christian speech, then, by definition, we cannot distinguish the voice of Jesus from the voice of the church, and therefore the search for the historical Jesus is futile. So if you accept the viability of historical Jesus research, you cannot avoid the criterion of distinctiveness.

Most everyone agrees that some version of this criterion is especially helpful in principle, but applying it can prove troublesome in concrete cases. The criterion produces minimalist results; it cannot do otherwise. Jesus said and did more than what is historically verifiable with this criterion. The vexing problem is how we move beyond this minimum to include material that is not distinctive. The Seminar is divided on this question. For us it comes down to how we regard the material we've colored gray. The Seminar assigns two meanings to the gray vote, which can be either a negative or a positive assessment of an item's historical authenticity.* If you consult the voting results, you can see that for many items colored gray there was a considerable percentage of red and pink votes.[35]

The Seminar has colored a lot of material gray. Many members of the Seminar, myself included, treat the gray material as a fund from which to expand the database for the historical Jesus beyond the red and pink minimum. The only items excluded in principle from the database are those colored black. Gray items can be considered on a case-by-case basis. This means that the working data base for many of us is substantially larger than the 18% of the sayings that are red and pink. This figure of 18% has gotten a lot of attention and all critics use it to show how skeptical the Seminar is. But consider what this 18% is 18% of. The ninety red and pink sayings are 18% of *all* the sayings attributed to Jesus in *all* Christian texts from the first three centuries, including gospels the Seminar unanimously voted black in their entirety, such as the Dialogue of the Savior, the Apocryphon of James, the Gospel of Mary, and the Infancy Gospel of Thomas. Regarding the Gospel of John, I believe it is fair to say that most scholars outside the Seminar would agree with us that few, if any, sayings in it are demonstrably authentic. So, if we set the range of the data base to be the sayings in Matthew, Mark, Luke, and Thomas, and if we realize that a good deal of the gray material can be included, the percentage of sayings in the data base is significantly larger than 18%. My conservative guess is that it is probably around 50% for most of us and even higher for some.

POLEMIC

The last issue I wish to address has to do not with the content of scholarship, but the conduct of scholars. As you may have noticed from the quotations excerpted in this chapter, some critics of the Seminar denounce it in language that is rancorous and sometimes venomous. The polemical rhetoric of these critics is the ugliest I have ever encountered in scholarly writing.

The operative assumption of these scholars and of the editorial committees who approve their writing for publication is that it is proper not only to attack opponent's ideas but also to insult them personally, to impugn their

---

* For an explanation of the ambiguity and uncertainty built into the gray vote, see pp. 52–53.

intellectual honesty, their moral integrity, and even their religious commitments. Perhaps I am saddened more than others by this verbal abuse because I belong to the group at which it is aimed. So I leave it to you to decide whether language like this brings shame on those at whom it is directed or on those from whom it comes.

The pettiness and nastiness of some of the criticisms of the Seminar shows that the Seminar's work has drilled into a nerve. The issues at stake are more than academic and it is natural that many have strong feelings about them. That is no excuse, however, for debasing the discussion with personal attacks. The spectacle of biblical scholars slinging mud at one another may be entertaining to some, but incivility in scholarly discourse distracts attention and energy from the real task, that of increasing our understanding.

I trust that everyone in the historical Jesus debate, regardless of his or her religious beliefs, sincerely desires to increase our understanding of Jesus and does so out of respect for him and what he has left us. Jesus' teaching is unambiguous about how we should relate to opponents. Honest disagreement is not to be avoided, for it can lead to greater understanding. What we disagree about is indeed important, but so is how we disagree. I hope we can conduct this debate about Jesus in a manner that honors his teaching and his memory.

CHAPTER FIVE

History is Not Optional

A Critique of *The Real Jesus* (I)

The most significant development in biblical scholarship over the past two decades has been the resurgence of interest in the historical Jesus. It has generated a vigorous debate that has spilled out of the usual academic venues, where it would otherwise still be proceeding in obscurity, and into the public arena. The national print media, sensing its potential for controversy, have paid close attention to it. For example, the 1996 Easter week issues of *Time, Newsweek*, and *U.S. News & World Report* all featured cover stories on the scholarly debate about the resurrection. Until recently the media took virtually no notice of the Bible (apart from bogus tabloid reports on such things as the alleged discovery of Noah's ark) and even less of serious biblical scholarship.

Journalism about the new Jesus scholarship consistently spotlights the disagreements among scholars and can foster the impression that the experts cancel each other out. Popular books on the historical Jesus amply demonstrate that there is little consensus among biblical scholars. Those who follow the historical Jesus debate from the sidelines may find it fascinating but also a bit bewildering. But it is not only the deadlock among scholars that can confuse the public; Christian observers of the debate may well be scandalized by what they hear or read. Many Christians are disconcerted, to say the least, when some of their cherished beliefs about Jesus, long considered non-negotiable in orthodox Christianity, are publicly called into question by credentialed biblical scholars, many of them on the faculties of Christian colleges and seminaries. Several theologically conservative scholars have weighed in with books that criticize the work of more liberal scholars and present portraits of the historical Jesus that leave orthodox beliefs unchallenged. Prominent among these apologetic studies is Luke Timothy Johnson's *The Real Jesus* (San Francisco: HarperSanFrancisco, 1996). Vigorously attacking scholars who (in the jargon of the Catholic magisterium) "scandalize the faithful" and taking an unqualified stand on the

This chapter is slightly revised from its original publication in *Biblical Theology Bulletin* 28 (1998), pp. 27–34, © Biblical Theology Bulletin. I regret the intemperance of some of my remarks in that article and trust that the present chapter is a calmer response to Professor Johnson.

canon and the creed, Johnson's book has been hailed as a powerful response to the troubling claims emerging from the historical Jesus debate.[1]

Johnson does not present himself as a participant in this debate, but rather as its adjudicator. So although the book deals with the discussion about the historical Jesus, it is not really intended to contribute to it. Johnson's goal for this book is much more ambitious. He hopes his book will put an end to the debate once and for all.

The book's subtitle is *The Misguided Quest for the Historical Jesus and the Truth of the Traditional Gospels*, the first half of which sums up one of its theses: that all attempts at historical reconstruction of the life and teachings of Jesus are doomed to failure. Johnson makes this case by criticizing recent Jesus books and by arguing that the New Testament writings cannot yield reliable historical information about Jesus beyond a few biographical facts.

In this chapter I analyze and respond to four elements of Johnson's argument: his polemical rhetoric, his specific criticisms of current historical Jesus research, his rejection of the historical value of the gospels, and his claim that the rise of Christianity cannot be explained historically.

JOHNSON'S POLEMICAL RHETORIC

Johnson's criticism of recent Jesus scholarship is unabashedly polemical. His writing about those he criticizes is laced with derision, contempt, and insulting insinuations.* Those who believe that academic discourse should debate ideas without personal polemic can decide for themselves whether Johnson's rhetoric discredits him or his opponents.

Johnson targets the historical Jesus books of Barbara Thiering, A. N. Wilson, Bishop Spong, and Stephen Mitchell (works not considered scholarly by the vast majority of biblical scholars), as well as the work of "three genuine academicians:" Marcus Borg, John Dominic Crossan, and Burton Mack (and later of John Meier, whom he respectfully criticizes). He also remarks dismissively on the work of James Robinson, Helmut Koester, Raymond Brown, and others, including even Edward Schillebeeckx. Johnson saves his most contemptuous remarks for the Jesus Seminar and Robert Funk, its *"magister ludi"* (p. 13). Indeed, the Jesus Seminar is what prompted Johnson to write this book, for he sees it "as a symptom of a deeper and more disturbing institutional collapse" (p. v).

---

* I remain stumped by Johnson's disclaimer in his Preface: "Although my views in this book are outspoken, I hope that my language is courteous" (p. vi). Readers can judge for themselves what standards of courtesy are evident in his writing.

Before taking up Johnson's critique of these books and their authors, we need to examine his polemical rhetoric, because it helps us understand the authorial stance he takes and the relationship it sets up between author and reader. Johnson presents himself throughout as a voice of sanity in a crowd of fools. His book comes across as a level-headed answer to a flood of silly, pretentious, fraudulent, and stupid writings on Jesus from both empty-headed amateurs and incompetent and dishonest scholars. I bring this up not to mourn Johnson's lack of charity, which, though lamentable, has nothing to do with whether his arguments are valid. I bring it up because Johnson's self-image as the authority figure is a central aspect of his rhetorical strategy. Johnson writes not only against books on the historical Jesus, but against historical-critical scholarship in general, which he regards as an experiment gone bad. He wants to persuade Christians that the study of the Bible should be re-subordinated to the theological, catechetical, and homiletic programs of traditional, mainline Christianity. To succeed in this he must convince readers that not only the quest for the historical Jesus, but the entire historical-critical model in which it is rooted, is intellectually misguided and religiously dangerous.

Johnson goes at this task by insinuating that much recent historical-critical scholarship is foolish. To take a specific example, we can consider his manner of assessing scholarship on Q. Johnson explains that most scholars accept the existence of Q, but until recently they "tended to a benign agnosticism concerning its precise dimensions or provenance" (p. 52). The paragraph that follows this statement is worth analyzing because it is a representative example of how Johnson's polemical rhetoric serves to *dismiss* scholarly work of which he disapproves.

> But in recent years, some scholars (such as Helmut Koester, James Robinson, Richard Edwards, and John Kloppenborg) pushed past such resistance to treat Q as if it were a specific, determinable composition rather than a convenient designation for a body of shared material. Many other scholars have taken up the chase, and there is even a Q Seminar of the Society of Biblical Literature that combs through these verses in search of redactional layers and other arcana (p. 52).

Note that Johnson does not actually assert that it is wrong to aim for precision about Q, much less does he say *why* it would be wrong. Instead, he relies on a condescending rhetoric. The "pushed past such resistance," "as if it were," "taken up the chase," "even," and "arcana" are unmistakably dismissive. Without actually claiming that these scholars are mistaken, the mild ridicule insinuates that such pursuits are so obviously wrongheaded that one need only describe them to expose their stupidity. Readers unfamiliar with these Q studies are given no hint of either the comprehensive scope or impressive erudition of the work Johnson dismisses. Nor are they made aware of the self-critical methodological reflection that characterizes the best of this work.

Instead of actually making an argument, Johnson exchanges knowing smiles with his readers, assuring them that they can safely ignore any scholarship whose results go beyond what he determines to be common sense. For lay readers this can be heady stuff, for it encourages them to sit in judgment on scholars and their pathetic endeavors. Described by the professorial blurbs on the dust jacket as a "seasoned and serious scholar" whose own work is "clear-headed" and "sober," Johnson comes across as someone who exposes how the Jesus Seminar, Borg, Crossan, Mack, and others substitute seductive rhetoric for argument, evidence, and logic. The irony of this "critique" has clearly escaped its author.

Polemical rhetoric can be annoying, to be sure, but can be bracketed out if accompanied by careful argument. With Johnson, however, the harshness of his attacks often serves to draw attention away from a lack of substance in his argument. The vigor of his polemical rhetoric can create the impression of a devastating critique. However, on page after page, after you sift through his rhetoric, you find that there is not much left. The paragraph on Q research quoted above is not some aberration; it represents the general tenor of the whole book.

JOHNSON'S CRITIQUE OF RECENT RESEARCH ON JESUS

In chapter 2, Johnson criticizes books by a broad spectrum of authors: Thiering, Spong, Mitchell, Wilson, Borg, Crossan, Mack, and the Jesus Seminar. In a concluding summary (pp. 54–55) he lists six of their "constant traits," all of which are obviously meant as criticisms.

1. These authors "reject canonical gospels as reliable sources for our knowledge of Jesus."
2. They reconstruct the historical Jesus "without reference to other canonical sources." (Johnson refers to Acts, the letters of Paul, Hebrews, 1 Peter, and James.)
3. They portray the mission of Jesus and his movement "in terms of a social or cultural critique rather than in terms of religious or spiritual realities."

4. They all have a theological agenda, inasmuch as they "want their understanding of Jesus and Christian origins to have an impact on Christians."

5. They assume that "historical knowledge is normative for faith, and therefore for theology" and that the "origins (of Christianity) define (its) essence."

6. Although the authors (except Mitchell) "have some form of identification with Christianity," their real allegiance is to academia.

Since these criticisms go to the heart of what Johnson thinks is misguided about historical Jesus research, they should be examined critically so as to assess their validity.

1. It is not clear what Johnson means by the claim that these authors "reject the canonical gospels as reliable sources for our knowledge of Jesus." At one level, this claim is patently false, because all these authors rely on the canonical gospels for their information about Jesus. Material found in Mark, Matthew, and Luke makes up virtually the entire data base for historical reconstructions of Jesus. The authors make limited use of the Gospel of Thomas as well, but almost always to reinforce parallel material from the canonical gospels.* Perhaps Johnson is complaining about their use of Q, but this would make little sense because all of Q is found in Matthew and Luke.

On the other hand, Johnson may mean that the authors reject the historical reliability of the narrative framework of the gospels. If so, he is right. But then so does Johnson. The irony is that Johnson is far more skeptical about the historical reliability of the gospels than any of those he criticizes. He attacks these authors precisely for their willingness to make historical inferences from gospel material that he regards as historically unreliable. For example, Johnson rejects using the parables to reconstruct Jesus' teaching because he doubts that any of them can be reliably traced to Jesus (p. 124).

The accusation that our authors "reject the canonical gospels as reliable sources for our knowledge of Jesus" is powerful rhetoric, but its power rides on its vagueness. When we try to ascertain exactly what it means, it turns out to be either false or something of which Johnson is more guilty than those he criticizes.

2. It is by and large true that the authors in question "reconstruct the historical Jesus without reference to canonical writings outside the gospels."

---

* On the Jesus Seminar's use of Thomas to bolster confidence in the historicity of numerous sayings in the canonical gospels, see pp. 70–71.

But there is a perfectly good reason for this: these works say very little about the pre-Easter Jesus. After sifting through the letters of Paul, 1 Peter, James, and Hebrews for statements about the historical Jesus, Johnson comes up with a list of seventeen items.

1. Jesus was a human person.
2. Jesus was a Jew.
3. Jesus was of the tribe of Judah.
4. Jesus was a descendant of David.
5. Jesus' mission was to the Jews.
6. Jesus was a teacher.
7. Jesus was tested.
8. Jesus prayed using the word *abba*.
9. Jesus prayed for deliverance from death.
10. Jesus suffered.
11. Jesus interpreted his last meal with reference to his death.
12. Jesus underwent a trial.
13. Jesus appeared before Pontius Pilate.
14. Jesus' end involved some Jews.
15. Jesus was crucified.
16. Jesus was buried.
17. Jesus appeared to witnesses after his death.

It is useful to compile such a list, if only to see how seldom the New Testament epistles refer to the pre-Calvary Jesus. The problem is that Johnson writes as if he has mapped out some dark continent of data, of which others are unaware. In reality, Johnson's list is merely an uncritical compilation. It provides no historical information that is not more amply available in the gospels, and Johnson acknowledges that not all of it is historically reliable (p. 122). Johnson needn't be "shocked" (p. 117) that recent Jesus studies slight this material.

3. The authors portray the mission of Jesus and his movement "in terms of a social or cultural critique rather than in terms of religious or spiritual realities."

Johnson should know better than to make this charge, for it assumes that "society" and "culture" are discrete categories opposed to "religion," a grossly inaccurate distinction for the ancient world (and one not very useful even in a secularized age like our own). If Johnson is seriously suggesting that to focus on the social and cultural aspects of life is to exclude religion, he would have to maintain that only a small part of the preaching of the likes of Amos, Micah, and Isaiah was religious, inasmuch as most of it focused on

Israel's economic, political, military, and social behavior. Seven of the Ten Commandments are concerned with social realities and do not mention religion, yet they are a cornerstone of the Covenant. Judaism simply takes it for granted that every aspect of life is part of religion.

Besides, Jesus chose the overtly political term *kingdom* (as in "kindgom of God") as the banner for his mission. One has to ignore major portions of Jesus' teaching (such as the parables) to think that he looked at religion as something separate from society and culture.

4. The authors all have a theological agenda, inasmuch as they "want their understanding of Jesus and Christian origins to have an impact on Christians."

Borg, Crossan, and Mack do have theological agendas and they make no attempt to hide them. Does Johnson seriously intend this as a criticism? If having a theological agenda is sufficient to impeach one's work, then, obviously, Johnson's book is similarly endangered.

Johnson's warning might be needed if these authors denied having a theological agenda, or even if they simply kept silent about it. But, as Johnson shows, the agendas of these authors are in print for all to read. Relating historical investigations to theology is commonplace in Christian thought. The critical question is whether one's theological views are compatible with the historical reconstruction, or whether the historical findings are predetermined by one's theological commitments.

5. The authors assume that "historical knowledge is normative for faith, and therefore for theology" and that the "origins [of Christianity] define [its] essence."

Here Johnson raises an important point. Quests for the historical Jesus almost always presuppose that Jesus got it right and the church messed it up, which is a bias rooted in the very structure of Protestant theology. Perhaps Johnson's Catholic sensibility makes him more alert to the arbitrariness of the assumption that "the original form of the Jesus movement was naturally better than any of its developments" (p. 55). But what if we treat this as a considered judgment rather than an a priori assumption? Among the disappointing developments in early Christianity are its anti-Semitism and the Church's collaboration with Roman imperial power. Nearly everyone regards these developments as corruptions of what Jesus stood for. Unless one wants to trace them to the historical Jesus, one is struck by the differences between Jesus and some later developments, and value judgments are unavoidable.

A deeper problem here for Johnson is that he too assumes that "origins define essence." It's just that he locates the origin of Christianity not in the historical Jesus, but in the risen Christ of the theological tradition that he regards as normative for Christianity. That Johnson does not reject the principle that "origins define essence" can be seen in the fact that he does not allow for even the possibility that the work of Crossan, Mack, Spong, and company might represent a providential development in Christianity. Johnson's assumption that origins define essence is fundamental to his project. When he advocates faithfulness to tradition he assumes it to be self-evidently true that Christians should do as he believes they have always done: shape their faith after the faith expressed in the canonical tradition. But this can be true only if Christianity's essence is defined by its origins.

6. Although the authors (except Mitchell) "have some form of identification with Christianity," their real allegiance is to academia.

Johnson claims that our authors' agenda amounts to "a demand for the dismantling of traditional Christian views" (Johnson's hyperbolic caricature for their invitation to understand Jesus historically rather than mythically). While he would expect such a "demand" from "outsiders," he is surprised that it should come from Christian scholars (though he carefully avoids admitting that they really are Christians—only that they "have some form of identification with Christianity"). Johnson needn't be so surprised. Calls for revision nearly always come from within. Peering into the souls of these authors, Johnson somehow discerns that their commitment to Christianity "is less strong than that professed toward scholarship" (p. 55). What offends Johnson is that they want their understanding of Jesus to make a difference in the church and not merely in the academy. Why is this wrong for them but right for Johnson, who wants the same thing? Unless this is brazen hypocrisy (which I assume it is not), it can only be because Johnson sees them as outsiders[2] and himself as an insider.

> If there is a "church" whose rules and rituals are home to these authors, it is that of the academy. The ideals espoused in this "church" provide the perspective for the criticism of the Christian "Church," which in all these discussions appears only as a problem and never as a mystery, always as a tragic mistake and never as a providential development (pp. 55–56).

Once again, Johnson's rhetoric obfuscates the issue. The effectiveness of his insider/outsider rhetoric depends on the reader's willingness to accept Johnson's judgment on the ultimate loyalties of people he does not know.*

---

* Johnson tells us on p. vi that before he completed his book, he personally knew only one of the authors he criticized.

Furthermore, his accusation that they use the standards of the academy to criticize the church is plainly false:* they all use the teachings of *the historical Jesus* as an ideal for movements claiming his name.

A deeper issue underlying Johnson's attack has to do with the relationship of critical biblical scholarship to the academy and the church, both of whom view it with some degree of suspicion. From within the academy, Johnson's charge against his colleagues is highly peculiar: scholars usually criticize the work of their colleagues on the grounds that it does not meet the high standards of academic discourse. Biblical scholars are criticized when their conclusions seem more rooted in theological pre-commitments than in a thoroughly critical assessment of the evidence. But here, Johnson castigates other scholars precisely for their commitment to the ideals of critical understanding. Johnson leaves no room for a dual commitment both to rigorous academic standards and to Christian tradition. That this dual allegiance can be difficult is not to be doubted. Johnson, however, insists that one must choose *between* Christianity and the academy. That is why he admonishes his fellow seminary professors that they should "take less seriously the judgment of our academic colleagues and more seriously the judgment of God" (p. 170). It is wise to be wary of those who want to be accountable to God and not to their peers.

Conclusions about Johnson's Critique

Johnson's criticisms of his opponents have little substance and less merit. Criticism 1 is either an error or a stone thrown from a glass house. Criticism 2 is true but unimportant. Criticism 3 sets up a false dichotomy. Criticisms 4 and 5 fault others for doing what Johnson himself does. Criticism 6 is unverifiable and downright peculiar. While the rhetoric of these criticisms is forceful, the argument is weak. The rhetoric seems to appeal, at least in part, to readers' emotions: to their affection for a venerated tradition and to resentment toward those who question it.

It is difficult to imagine how readers who have studied the authors in question could give much credence to Johnson's critique. Instead of encouraging honest critical inquiry without prior conditions, Johnson assures his audience that they need not bother to read the authors he attacks. "Poisoning the well" is an old debating trick which, like all tricks, aims to fool rather than to persuade.

---

* Johnson knows this and criticizes them for it in the preceeding paragraph on p. 55—see item 5 above.

HISTORY, MEANING, AND THE GOSPELS

Johnson argues in chapters 4 and 5 that very little in the gospels ("only an extraordinarily limited amount of information" [p. 108]) can be shown to be historical. He does not identify a single saying of Jesus that he considers historically authentic. However, he does maintain that a few general facts about Jesus can be established (for example, that he was a Jewish teacher and healer who was crucified under Pilate).

In chapter 5 Johnson argues that facts by themselves cannot yield meanings. He emphasizes that even though we can be sure of a very few facts about Jesus, we cannot know what they mean. This is because facts have meaning only in context with other facts and within larger patterns of meanings (narratives). Without a narrative framework, the facts identified by historians remain discrete items. "It is *not* legitimate on the basis of demonstrating the probability of such items to connect them, arrange them in sequence, infer causality, or ascribe special significance to any combination of them" (pp. 124–25). Johnson argues that if we reject the historical reliability of the gospel narratives (and he holds that we must), then we have no historical framework at all for interpreting the meaning of the words and deeds of Jesus.

Johnson especially objects to the use of models from the social sciences as frameworks for interpretation and he attacks Borg and Crossan on this point (pp. 42, 45–46, 125). Two responses to Johnson's objection can be registered in passing. 1) The use of models of culture in biblical interpretation is not optional. The choice is not *whether* to use such models, but *which* ones to use. Those who do not consciously choose one or who deny they need one end up reading the assumptions of their own culture into the Bible. 2) Johnson seems to refute himself in his epilogue, where he argues that "the writers of the New Testament were not Trobrianders" (p. 173) and so must be understood in their cultural "otherness." This seems inconsistent with his earlier condemnation of Borg and Crossan. If this is not an inconsistency, Johnson must implicitly be making a very fine distinction: we need cultural models (and if they don't come from the social sciences, then from where?) for interpreting the texts, but it it illegitimate to use these models for historical reconstruction. Unfortunately, Johnson does not elaborate.

Johnson would have us use the gospel narratives or nothing at all, because apart from them there are no controls: "All such constructions [of the historical Jesus] lack any real claim to historical probability once the given narrative framework has definitively been abandoned" (p. 125). It is important that we not misunderstand Johnson here: he is *not* asserting that the narrative frameworks of the gospels are historical—he argues against this at length. His point is that *we do not know, and in principle cannot know, with any acceptable degree of probability, what the historical Jesus meant by his teachings or intended by his deeds.* For example, Johnson maintains that even if we could be sure that Jesus taught in parables (and he claims that we cannot), we still could not tell what Jesus meant by them (p. 133).

Johnson drives home the crucial distinction between what someone says and what someone means. What is said can, in principle, be recovered historically, but what is meant is available only through "narrative" (understood in a general sense as a pattern of interpretation). Now what happens if we apply this principle not only to the historical Jesus, but to the gospels themselves? We know what they "say," but we cannot know what they mean, except within a "narrative." But which narrative? For Johnson, this narrative is the pattern supplied by the canon and the creed, which is for him the authoritative framework for interpreting the gospels.

One may choose to interpret the gospels within the "narrative" (the pattern of meaning) of canon and creed, but only at the price of sacrificing historical clarity, because canon and creed are faith statements of the fourth century, and were intentionally formulated to control the interpretation of the gospels. Canon-and-creed is the appropriate interpretive framework *if* the goal is to understand the meaning of the gospels from the perspective of the fourth-century Christian authorities who had gained ascendancy in the Roman Empire and who sought to define what counts as legitimate Christianity. But if the goal is to understand the meaning of the gospels against the background of their own historical context, then, by definition, the history of *first*-century Christianity is the "story" within which these texts have their meaning. Johnson maintains that the nature of the evidence allows us to know far too little about this story for it to serve the needs of responsible historiography. He actually mocks the attempt to reconstruct the history of first-century Christianity as "a paper chase, pure and simple . . . like a house of cards . . . *There are no controls*; there is only imagination hitched to an obsessive need, somehow, anyhow, to do 'history'" (pp. 99–100).

It is good for Johnson to remind us how fragile and incomplete our knowledge of this history is, but his contemptuous dismissal is not the only, nor even the most obvious, assessment. Johnson presents himself as a voice of moderation, but his position is extreme. Most scholars, whether they be conservative or liberal theologically, or even non-theological in their orientation, find it possible to draw significant historical conclusions from the evidence. There are vigorous debates over which historical reconstructions are best supported by the evidence, but there is widespread agreement that specific and important conclusions can be drawn. Scholars who are circumspect about their methods realize that historical conclusions about early Christianity should be drawn with caution and held with humility. Johnson is right to warn us of the uncertainty inherent in reconstructing early Christian history, but he is wrong to write off the entire project as intellectually bankrupt.

CAN THE RISE OF CHRISTIANITY BE EXPLAINED HISTORICALLY?

One might choose to join Johnson in rejecting history as an interpretive framework in favor of an ahistorical (or mythic) framework, which is what Johnson does in asserting that the resurrection is "the necessary and sufficient cause" of the rise of early Christianity (p. 136). But recourse to the resurrection as the explanation for Christianity does not deliver one from the circularity that Johnson denounces in the effort to reconstruct the history of early Christianity from its writings. The circle is still there: the resurrection is the myth of origins *in* the New Testament texts that then is used as the explanation for the origin *of* the New Testament.[3]

Johnson affirms that the resurrection is not an historical event (p. 140). For him this does not mean that the resurrection did not happen. Rather, it means that it is a supernatural reality beyond human history, which is why he denounces the "insistence on reducing the resurrection to something 'historical'"(p. 139). Along with the vast majority of theologians and biblical scholars, he holds that the supernatural reality of the resurrection cannot be deduced from the historical evidence.* He also insists, however, that unless we have faith in a miraculous resurrection, we will not realize that it is the necessary and sufficient cause of the rise of early Christianity. "The effort to reduce the resurrection experience to just another historical element runs the risk of failing to account for the rise of the historical movement" (p. 139). Johnson thus maintains that the rise of this historical movement cannot be explained historically. That is why the explanation (the resurrection experience) has to be ahistorical, that is, a divine miracle.

This appeal to divine intervention to explain the origins of a religion is a common apologetical strategy. Jewish apologists argue that their people would have disappeared long ago if their history was not divinely guided. Muslim apologists argue that the rapid and widespread acceptance of

---

* See my discussion on pp. 141–46.

monotheism by the pagan Arabs could not have occurred unless Islam was truly from God. Baha'i apologists argue that the worldwide spread of their faith despite the fierce persecution of its founders and early members testifies to its divine authority. And Christian apologists argue that the rise of early Christianity defies "merely" historical explanation. Johnson is clearly attempting to pre-empt explanations incompatible with the doctrinal orthodoxy he defends: that the rise of Christianity is a miracle beyond human explanation, and so its very existence proves its supernatural origins.

Johnson's insistence that the resurrection is beyond history is really a way of declaring it off-limits to historical inquiry. This tactic is by no means unique to Johnson. It is fairly common among New Testament scholars, many of whom apply historical criticism to the rest of the gospels, but wish to shield the resurrection stories from rigorous historical scrutiny. In the case of these scholars, it is puzzling why a critical method that helps them understand the rest of the gospels should not be used on their final chapters. Johnson's position, however, is not burdened by this inconsistency, for it is not the case that he endorses the historical-critical method in general but disallows its use on the resurrection texts. No, he rejects historical criticism in its entirety.

It's not as if Johnson is against interpreting the Bible critically. In the ten-page epilogue to his book, "Critical Scholarship and the Church," Johnson sketches "the possibilities for a truly critical biblical scholarship within a Church that is also faithful to its Lord" (p. 168). Johnson is emphatically not anti-intellectual and has little use for conservative scholarship that "is critical in form much more than in substance," and that uses "the paraphernalia of the academy—often with considerable cleverness—to support conclusions already determined by doctrine" (p. 63). Johnson assures us that he is committed to "truly critical biblical scholarship." His quarrel is with *histori-cal*-critical scholarship, the "hegemony" of which has produced "several generations of scholars and theologians (who) have been disabled from direct and responsible engagement with the texts of the tradition in their religious dimension" (p. 169).4

Johnson's criticism of the historical-critical model of biblical scholarship unfolds in his chapter 4, "The Limits of History," which aims to bring some theoretical sophistication to a pre-critical understanding of the concept of history. His basic point is that since all history is reconstruction, its results are never certain, but only more or less probable. This, of course, is nothing new and is taken for granted by all scholars who are not fundamentalist or evangelical. Johnson complains that historical Jesus books seldom explain this sufficiently, letting readers' naive positivist assumptions go unchallenged. Johnson's point, though not original, has some validity.5

What spoils Johnson's case is that he casts the net far too broadly, imply-ing that since historical reconstructions are all hypothetical and therefore at best highly probable, the very task of historical reconstruction is misguided. (Recall the subtitle of his book: *The Misguided Quest for the Historical Jesus*.) Underneath all this is a longing for an unshakeable certainty on which to establish Christian faith. This kind of certainty is unavailable in reconstruc-tions of the history of Jesus or of early Christianity, indeed in any knowledge produced by historical criticism. So Johnson rejects the historical-critical method and pleads for an interpretation of the New Testament controlled by the doctrines of the Church. This method of interpretation makes it easy to believe that Christian faith is based on a divine revelation untainted by the imperfections of humanly constructed knowledge.

The critical study of the historical Jesus raises a host of questions, some of them "dangerous" to traditional orthodoxy, and it does not give absolutely certain answers. The risk is real: the historical Jesus just might lead us to rethink some fundamental Christian beliefs. Johnson's advice is that we should call off the search for the historical Jesus before it's too late.

CHAPTER SIX

The Jesus of Orthodoxy
and the Jesuses of Gospels

A Critique of *The Real Jesus* (II)

This chapter continues my critique of Johnson's book. The preceding chapter examined Johnson's explication of the first part of his book's subtitle: *The Misguided Quest for the Historical Jesus.* A central thesis of the book is that all attempts at historical reconstruction of the life and teachings of Jesus are doomed to fail. Johnson supports this thesis in three ways: 1) by criticizing recent books on the historical Jesus; 2) by trying to show that the gospels cannot yield objective historical information about Jesus beyond a few biographical facts; and 3) by arguing that the historical Jesus is irrelevant to Christian belief and practice.

Although *The Real Jesus* presents itself as a reasoned refutation of recent historical Jesus research, I argued in the preceding chapter that in reality this book is a deeply flawed and extremist defense of Christian orthodoxy. My critique analyzed four aspects of Johnson's argument.

1. The harshness of Johnson's polemics create the impression of a power-ful critique, but serve mainly to distract the reader from the lack of sub-stance in his arguments.
2. Johnson's specific criticisms of recent historical Jesus books are very weak and seemed designed to play on readers' emotions.
3. Johnson believes that the search for the historical Jesus is misguided because, in his view, the gospels are virtually worthless historically. This is an extremist position rejected by the vast majority of biblical scholars.
4. Johnson's position that early Christianity can only be explained by a miracle (the resurrection) is transparently apologetical. Johnson attempts to protect the traditional theological picture of Christian origins by declaring it off-limits to historical-critical inquiry.

In this chapter I take up the second of Johnson's two major theses. This thesis, captioned by the second half of the book's subtitle (*The Truth of the*

This chapter is slightly revised from its original publication in the *Journal for the Study of the New Testament* 68 (1997), pp. 101–20. Reproduced by permission of Sheffield Academic Press Limited. I wish to thank Roy Hoover for this careful attention to an earlier draft of this chapter and his judi-cious suggestions that have improved it.

Traditional Gospels), is that the canonical gospels convey the true meaning of Jesus' life and death. Johnson supports this thesis by arguing that: 1) Christian faith is grounded, not in the historical Jesus, but in the resurrected Jesus experienced by his followers (what Johnson calls "the real Jesus"); 2) the early Christian understanding of this "real" Jesus is communicated in the "traditional gospels;" and 3) Christian life should be modeled after the meaning of Jesus' existence revealed by the pattern of his life found in the canonical gospels.

I focus my critique on Johnson's distinctive construal of "the truth of the traditional gospels". My response is in three parts. First, I examine Johnson's position on the relationship of faith to history. Then, in the major portion of this chapter, I criticize Johnson's theory that the canonical gospels all present the meaning of Jesus' life according to a single pattern. I go about this by comparing the pattern Johnson proposes to the evidence we find in the synoptic gospels. I conclude by contesting the particular kind of truth Johnson claims for the traditional gospels.

FAITH AND HISTORY IN THE GOSPELS

In chapter 6 of his book, "The Real Jesus and the Gospels," Johnson argues that a pattern of Jesus' life (an interpretive framework within which his life has meaning) "was embedded in the earliest Christian experience *and memory* faithfully mirrored in the Gospel narrative" (p. 152, emphasis added). Johnson is careful not to claim that this pattern is accurate historically, lest he be on a "misguided" quest for the historical Jesus. Nonetheless, his use of the word "memory" constitutes an implicit attempt to do just that. To imply that this pattern, forged out of Christian religious experience, is also rooted in memories of what Jesus said and did prior to the cross is to harvest the fruit of history without doing the hard work of historical reconstruction. Johnson tries to have his cake and eat it too. He can focus on belief in the resurrection as something that makes all the difference in how Jesus' followers interpreted the meaning of his life and person. He can also assert with equal conviction that it makes no real difference at all because the pattern of Jesus' life that emerges in light of belief in his resurrection is embedded in memories about the historical Jesus. This obviously begs the central question of whether the historical construct known as "Jesus as he was during his life in Palestine" is the same as the religious construct known as "Jesus as experienced by those who believe in his resurrection." To discern the first we hunt for *memory*. To discern the second we analyze religious *experience*. By claiming that the pattern of Jesus' life that he describes is based on "the earliest Christian experience *and* memory," Johnson elides the two.

The phrase "and memory," even if it is a careless slip rather than a strategic insinuation, is more important than its incidental placement may indicate. It shows that even Johnson wants a portrait of Jesus that he can consider historically accurate. My "even" reflects the fact that Johnson carefully argues that historical portraits of Jesus should be irrelevant to Christian belief and that the essential character of Christian life is determined by the response to the risen ("real") Jesus, not to the historical Jesus (the "unreal" Jesus?). Johnson is thus in the position to leave unanswered the whole question of memory (the historical accuracy of reports about the words and deeds of Jesus). He can leave it unanswered because he argues that it is unanswerable, except in extremely general terms. And yet, in a crucial sentence setting out an important thesis we find "memory" anchoring the issue in the historical Jesus.

Why is historicity important, even to someone who eloquently claims that it isn't? Johnson's personal motivation is irrelevant; what is important is the structural issue of the relationship of faith to history. The sentence immediately prior to the one with "and memory" in it is this one: "The really critical issue is this: are the pattern and meaning that the Gospels give to Jesus due simply to the artistry of one writer whom everyone else copied?" (pp. 151–52). The blatant way Johnson sets up the strawman here ("simply") highlights what is at stake in his question. What assurance is there that "the Gospel pattern"—and it is crucial for Johnson that there be only one—is based on the way Jesus "really" was and not on early Christian mythmaking or the creative imagination of a religious genius like Mark? At the end of the paragraph Johnson is arguing only that the pattern faithfully reflects post-Calvary Christian experience. But even if we grant this, the question of its connection to the historical Jesus remains unanswered. That is why it so important for Johnson to close the gap by asserting that the pattern is more than a distillation of religious experience or religious imagination; it is a reflection of *history* accessed through *memory*. At the bottom line it still matters whether the way early Christians experienced the risen Jesus has some identifiable continuity with the way Jesus was historically. Inescapably, for Christianity it very much matters what really happened.

What does Johnson mean by this "pattern"? It is an interpretive framework communicated in the gospel narratives. Johnson describes it as a "pattern of radical obedience to God and selfless love toward other people" (p. 158). For Johnson this pattern concerns both "the identity of Jesus and the character of discipleship" (p. 155). It thus has two interlinked functions. 1) It conveys the meaning of Jesus' life and death. 2) It establishes a paradigm for Christians to imitate. Johnson argues that this pattern is found in all four canonical gospels, and among the gospels, only in the canonical ones. He also maintains that this pattern is the only one common to all four New Testament gospels.[1]

We need to scrutinize Johnson's thesis by testing the adequacy of the pattern he proposes against a careful reading of the gospels. My analysis of the gospels will be more detailed than Johnson's because I aim to compare the very general terms in which he describes his pattern with the particularities of the individual gospels.* The following analysis demonstrates that if we allow the gospels to speak on their own terms, they do not manifest a single pattern. Though they reflect aspects of Johnson's pattern, they do so in very different configurations, and no one gospel actually contains the pattern Johnson describes. Johnson's pattern is not actually derived from the gospels, but rather is imposed on them.

THE JESUSES OF THE GOSPELS

The Markan Jesus

Johnson rightly maintains that "Mark deliberately shapes his image of Jesus according to a pattern of suffering in service to others, and shows that discipleship means following in that same pattern" (p. 154). What catches my attention is a small but significant difference in the way Johnson describes the pattern when he has four gospels in mind ("radical obedience to God *and* selfless love toward other people" [p. 158]) and how he describes it specifically in reference to Mark ("suffering *in* service to others" [p. 154]). Between the "and" in the first description and the "in" in the second there is a crucial difference: the first puts equal weight on both Jesus' death ("radical obedience") and his selfless service to others, whereas the second subsumes service into death (in effect, a death interpreted as service).

Whether or not this slippage is intentional on Johnson's part, his larger argument depends on gliding back and forth between these two notions as if they were equivalent. However, the difference between them makes a difference. The first describes a life of selfless love and obedience to God, but without mentioning the only referent this obedience has in Johnson's anal-

---

* I analyze Mark, Matthew, and Luke. These three gospels are more than sufficient for our purpose. Since Matthew and Luke copied from Mark, and since their patterns are quite different from Mark's, there is no need to belabor the point by analyzing John.

ysis: Jesus' submission to the death that God has decreed for him. On the other hand, the second describes only a willing martyrdom (that is, an obedient death that expresses selfless service) that is not necessarily preceded by a life of loving service to others. I focus on this difference because while it is beyond question that Mark's Jesus accepts his martyrdom in obedience to God, it is far from clear that Mark portrays Jesus' life as one of selfless love.

If we look for stories in Mark that show Jesus acting out of love for others, it is surprisingly difficult to find any. The exorcisms and healings in Mark can be taken as acts of love, but that is not how Mark seems to see them. We expect to find references to Jesus' love, or at least his compassion, in these stories (and we can find them in several of Luke's adaptations of them), but they simply are not in evidence in Mark.[2] The only occurrences of the word "love" in Mark are in 10:21, where Jesus loves the rich man, and in 10:29–31, where Jesus quotes the commandments to love God and neighbor. Mark interprets Jesus' healings and exorcisms as eschatological acts (3:23–27) and uses them to focus attention not on Jesus' love, but on his extraordinary *power*.

Let me be clear. The issue here is not what Jesus may have intended by his healings. According to the terms in which Johnson frames the problem, the issue is how Mark "deliberately shapes" the stories about Jesus' healings (p. 154). Let us assume that if we could somehow ask Mark personally, he would not deny that Jesus' miracles were deeds of loving mercy. But that is beside the point. The question here is into what pattern Mark has pressed this tradition of Jesus the wonder worker. My answer is the same as Johnson's: the pattern of Jesus the suffering Son of Man.

One might say that Jesus' miracles count as acts of selfless love because he performs them on behalf of others even though they put his life in danger. But this is not how Mark tells the story. It is not the exasperation of his enemies at his miracles that leads to his death.[3] On the surface of Mark's narrative, Jesus' enemies decide to kill him because of his extravagant claims about himself and his deliberate flaunting of Jewish traditions like the sabbath law (Mark 2:1–3:6). At a deeper level, however, Jesus' death for Mark is simply and mysteriously the fate God has decreed for him.*

Another problem with describing the Markan Jesus as a man of selfless love are the disturbing indications to the contrary, such as Jesus' disowning of his family (3:31–35), his declaration that those who accuse him of having an unclean spirit cannot ever be forgiven (3:28–30), and his strategy of

---

* See, for example, Jesus' prayer in Gethsemane (Mark 14:32–36) in which he accepts his gruesome death as the will of God, and his assertion that he "is destined" (*dei*) to be put to death in Mark 8:31.

teaching in parables so as to deliberately hide the meaning of his teaching from outsiders and thus deny them the opportunity for repentance and forgiveness (4:10–12).

Not only are very few of Jesus' deeds characterized by Mark as acts of selfless love; very little of Jesus' teaching has to do with loving or serving others. Johnson cites only two passages (9:35 and 10:43–45) that deal with service, and it is difficult to come up with any more than these.* When Jesus refers to his own service, it is in the context of his death (10:45). For Mark, *Jesus' death is his service:* his blood is "poured out for many" (14:24) and he "gives his life as a ransom for many" (10:45). Johnson is thus correct that Mark's portrait of Jesus is shaped by the pattern of suffering in service to others. Johnson is mistaken, however, when he later describes a pattern of suffering in obedience to God *and* selfless love toward others, because this implies that there is a pattern of selfless love in addition to one of martyrdom.

The difference between "suffering in service" and "suffering and service" is crucial because the whole point of Johnson's characterization of this pattern is that it sets up a paradigm of discipleship: being a Christian entails imitating the pattern of Jesus' life. This is exactly how Mark proceeds and it is unquestionably true that he defines discipleship in terms of one's willingness to suffer martyrdom for the sake of Jesus and the good news (8:34–35). Mark's Jesus lays down other non-negotiable demands, such as selling everything and giving it to the poor, abandoning one's family, and becoming the slave of others (Mark 10:21, 29–30, 43–44). Still, martyrdom is the primary aspect of discipleship for Mark. The exhortation to become the slave of others is a general one without reference to any specific incidents in the life of Jesus. (Which example in Mark of Jesus' enslavement to others is a disciple supposed to imitate?)

According to Mark one is true follower of Jesus only to the extent that one is prepared to be martyred in his name (8:33–35). For Mark's audience martyrdom was a real, if unlikely, possibility and so we can appreciate the uncompromising vision of discipleship with which Mark challenged his audience. The problem comes when Johnson claims that this pattern is still normative today. Contemporary governments (at least the ones under which most of Johnson's readers live) are not particularly interested in executing Christians. So if martyrdom is the measure of discipleship, what do you do when no one wants to kill you? The Markan pattern, horrifically relevant to Mark's situation, is now, thank God, obsolete.

---

* Mark 10:21 should probably be added. Here Jesus speaks to a rich man: "Sell what you own, give the money to the poor, and you will have treasure in heaven; then, come, follow me."

All this helps us see the logic by which Johnson's initial "suffering in service to others" (the pattern he perceives in Mark) turns into "radical obedience to God and selfless love toward other people" (the pattern he claims is common to all four canonical gospels).[4] If we take Mark's pattern *in the terms in which Mark expresses it*, there is little if anything for contemporary First World Christians to imitate. They can, of course, do what homiletic practice has done to Mark for centuries: make the pattern usable by redefining its terms of reference, treating "the cross" as a cipher for all manner of difficulties (from terminal diseases to annoying co-workers) rather than an unambiguously literal reference to death by crucifixion. But Johnson's transformation of the pattern is more subtle and more sweeping. He alters the Markan pattern in two ways, both of which are crucial if the pattern is to speak to a contemporary audience. 1) Mark's "martyrdom in obedience to God" becomes Johnson's "radical obedience to God." Readers can forget (and Johnson does not remind them) that the Markan Jesus' obedience to God is hammered out on the anvil of the cross. "Not my will but yours be done" (Mark 14:36) is not a generic expression of obedience but an anguished acceptance of a horrifying death. Johnson's "radical obedience to God" is thus abstracted from the specificity of Mark's narrative. 2) As analyzed above, Mark's "suffering in service to others" becomes Johnson's "selfless love toward other people." Johnson abandons the specifically Markan manner in which Jesus' service is portrayed in favor of a generic formulation of a universal human ideal.

Both of these modifications work in the same way: they remove the pattern from its Markan martyrological context. Johnson's final formulation of the pattern requires cutting it free from its roots in Mark's peculiar narrative. The irony in this is striking: Johnson's pattern no longer reflects what may be called "the historical Mark." It is a pattern that originates in Mark, but is given its concrete formulation, not by the specific contours of Mark's narrative, but by the context of the New Testament canon and the sensibilities of a modern audience. It is not Mark on Mark's own terms, but Mark as harmonized with three other gospels and adapted to a contemporary context. The result, though probably not the intent, of Johnson's harmonization and modernization of Mark is to render "the historical Mark" functionally irrelevant for Christian belief and practice.

Another irony has to do with Johnson's authorial stance within the scholarly debate. He roundly criticizes others for interpreting the meaning of Jesus within patterns not directly derived from the literary designs of the gospels.[5] Yet what Johnson does is no different from what he criticizes others for doing. He derives a pattern from Mark, but after he has traced it through

Matthew, Luke, John, and other New Testament texts, it emerges with its Markan martyrological coloring bleached out.

Given Johnson's project of describing a pattern that is attested in all four gospels, a result like this is inevitable, for the only kind of pattern that could be common to all four would have to be formulated at a high level of abstraction. "Obedience to God and selfless love for others" is such a generic pattern that it is difficult to think of religious heroes from any theistic tradition to whom it would *not* apply.

Johnson's inability to sustain a sharply focused pattern throughout the four gospels points to a deeper problem in his procedure. He begins with Mark and finds a pattern focused on Jesus as martyr. So far, so good. He then turns to Matthew and Luke to see if they retain Mark's pattern or if they eliminate it in favor of other patterns they impose. He correctly concludes that they take over Mark's pattern. But Johnson implies that Matthew and Luke do more than simply take it over—he gives the impression that the Markan pattern is somehow determinative for Matthew and Luke. Here is where the trouble begins. The pattern of Jesus as suffering Son of Man and the paradigm of discipleship as following the way of the martyr is the one that provides the literary structure and thematic unity of Mark, but this is not the case for Matthew and Luke.

The Matthean Jesus

Johnson claims that Matthew not only assimilates Mark's pattern into his own gospel, but also that he amplifies key elements in it. Given the brevity with which Johnson states his case (half a page), it is unrealistic to expect a comprehensive argument. Nevertheless, the evidence he presents is both selective and ambiguous. For example, he claims that Matthew "intensifies the picture of Jesus as suffering servant: he adds specific quotations from Torah [sic] that identify Jesus as the Isaian servant (Matt. 8:17; 12:18–21)" (p. 154). These quotations (which are from Isaiah, not the Torah) relate Jesus' status as suffering servant to his exorcisms and healings, not to his death. Thus, Matthew's use of these biblical texts show him altering Mark's distinctive emphasis on Jesus' martyrdom. That is, the evidence Johnson cites actually reveals how Matthew takes over Mark's basic concept only to reconfigure it. In fact, Matthew modifies Mark's pattern to such an extent that Matthew's version of this pattern can be harmonized with Mark's only by ignoring what is most recognizably Markan about it.

Johnson's assertion that Matthew takes up Mark's pattern and amplifies parts of it is, at some level of generality, correct. However, the impression created by Johnson that Matthew's portrait of Jesus is a more emphatic version of Mark's suffering Son of Man is quite wrong. If we consider the whole of Matthew's gospel, we see that the few passages Johnson selects from it to support his case are not well integrated into Matthew's overarching portrait of Jesus or his distinctive understanding of discipleship. Matthew's Jesus repeats the words of Mark's Jesus about his coming crucifixion and about the need for his followers to prepare for martyrdom. But the important difference is that for Mark this is the essence of Jesus' mission and the essence of discipleship, whereas for Matthew it is only part of the picture, and not the most important part. When we examine the places where Matthew develops his own understanding of the meaning of discipleship we find no mention either of martyrdom or the metaphor of slavery/service.

Let us consider three passages, all of them unique to the Gospel of Matthew and all of them located at crucial junctures in its literary structure: 1) at the conclusion of the Sermon on the Mount, Jesus' first and greatest discourse; 2) at the midpoint of the gospel, as Jesus concludes his middle discourse; 3) at the conclusion of the gospel as a whole. First, the Sermon on the Mount concludes with an exhortation about the need to put the teachings of Jesus into practice.

> Everyone then who hears these words of mine and acts on them will be like a wise man who built his house on rock. The rain fell, the floods came, and the winds blew and beat on that house, but it did not fall, because it had been founded on rock. And everyone who hears these words of mine and does not act on them will be like a foolish man who built his house on sand. The rain fell, the floods came, and the winds blew and beat against that house, and it fell—and great was its fall. (Matt 7:24–27)

Second, the pivotal discourse in Matthew (the third discourse out of five) is the collection of parables in chapter 13, all of them dealing with various aspects of the spreading of the good news. At the conclusion of these parables, Jesus asks,

> "Have you understood all this?" They answered, "Yes." And he said to them, "Therefore every scribe who has been trained for the kingdom of heaven is like the master of a household who brings out of his treasure what is new and what is old." (Matt 13:51–52)

Third, in the final passage in the gospel Jesus commissions the eleven disciples.

> Go therefore and make disciples of all nations, baptizing them in the name of the Father and of the Son and of the Holy Spirit, and teaching them to obey everything that I have commanded you. (Matt 28:19–20)

A comprehensive description of Matthew's pattern of discipleship would need to consider much more material, but these three passages are Matthew's own summary conclusions. They thus reveal what he wants to emphasize about the meaning of following Jesus: understanding Jesus' teaching, putting it into practice, and teaching others to do the same. The final words of this gospel are especially important and perfectly clear: Jesus sends out his disciples, not to serve and suffer, but to baptize and teach.

Yes, Matthew does reproduce Mark's material about disciples following Jesus on the way to the cross, but he neither emphasizes nor elaborates this aspect of discipleship and does not mention it at all in those passages that are distinctly Matthean. Matthew repeats this Markan material, but his real interest is in a different pattern of imitating Jesus.

What is true of Matthew's pattern of discipleship is also true of his portrait of Jesus. Matthew takes over Mark's pattern of Jesus as martyr, but goes on to develop his own pattern of Jesus as teacher-like-Moses.

So I do not deny what Johnson asserts: that we can find Mark's pattern replicated in Matthew. But we find it there altered and marginalized. If we respect the integrity of Matthew's gospel (that is, if we take Matthew on his own terms) rather than selecting only those elements that harmonize with Mark's agenda, we discover a complex and nuanced pattern, not all of the elements of which are easily integrated with each other.[6] Johnson does Matthew an injustice by his facile implication that Matthew is essentially an improved version of Mark.

The Lukan Jesus

Johnson makes a stronger claim about Luke's appropriation of Mark's pattern than he does about Matthew's. "The pattern of the suffering Messiah is, if anything, even more central to the plot of the two-volume work called Luke-Acts" (p. 155). Johnson's brief treatment of Luke suffers from the same problem as his treatment of Matthew. He identifies similarities between the Lukan and Markan patterns of Jesus, but ignores the differences, as if the differences make no real difference. However, if we look at the way Luke reshapes the Markan pattern, the differences are as important as the similarities. The major difference has to do with the most fundamental aspect of Mark's configuration: the equation of suffering with service, for as I argued above, Jesus' death is his service according to Mark. The most important Markan passage on this is Mark 10:45, which comes as the climactic pronouncement of the third passion prediction, where Jesus teaches that his death is a "ransom for many". So it is highly significant that Luke deletes just this phrase. That Luke objects to this specific verse is unmistakable because he reproduces the rest of the story to which it is the concluding statement (compare Mark 10:41–45 to Luke 22:24–27). If we ask why Luke declines to echo Mark's notion that Jesus' death was a ransom, we discover that Luke portrays Jesus not as a servant-martyr (as in Mark) but as a prophet-martyr.[7]

While this may seem a fine distinction, the difference it makes is important: a martyred servant dies *for* his people, but a martyred prophet is killed *by* his people. The death of a servant-martyr can be understood in some mysterious way (which, unfortunately, Mark never explains) to benefit others. But the murder of a prophet is a different matter, for it is a sign of the stubborn unrepentance of the people to whom the prophet is sent. Such a death benefits no one. On the contrary, it dooms those who do the killing, not so much because it is a murder, but because it is a rejection of God's message in the person of God's messenger. In Luke's view, Israel rejects Jesus just as it rejected all of God's messengers, but it is this final and definitive rejection that brings catastrophe on Israel (see Luke 13:34–35). In his gospel, Luke is careful not to lay blame for Jesus' death on Israel as a whole,[8] but it is the nation, especially Jerusalem, that suffers the consequences (see Jesus' warning to the "daughters of Jerusalem" in Luke 23:27–31). For Luke this is tragedy on a grand scale; hence the weeping, both by Jesus (19:41–44) and the women (23:27), and the sober and shaken reaction of the crowd that witnesses the crucifixion (23:48).

So Luke disagrees with Mark on the fundamental significance of the death of Jesus. According to Mark, Jesus dies because of his obedience to God; according to Luke, Jesus dies because of the disobedience of the people. The Markan Jesus comes to die; that is his mission. The Lukan Jesus comes to preach the prophets' message of repentance and ends up suffering the prophets' fate. For Mark the cross signals the "success" of Jesus' mission.* For Luke Jesus' death marks the failure of his mission and Israel's refusal of its last chance to repent, with tragic consequences for God's people.[9]

Johnson points out that in Luke-Acts the disciples suffer just like Jesus (p. 155), by which he implies that Luke promotes the same understanding of discipleship as Mark. But here also the differences are as interesting as the similarities. True, Luke reproduces Mark's demand that disciples carry their crosses just as Jesus carried his. However, Luke subverts the martyrological connotation of this grisly demand: Jesus' followers are to carry their crosses "daily" (Luke 9:23). Here the cross is no longer the literal instrument of imperial execution, but a symbol for all manner of hardship. You can be put

---

* See Mark's fascinating juxtaposition of the moment of Jesus' death with the portentous ripping of the temple curtain and the public recognition of Jesus' supernatural identity (Mark 15:37–39).

to death but once, whereas you can suffer rejection repeatedly. For Luke, disciples carry on Jesus' mission and, like him, are rejected by those to whom they preach. Yet in Acts only two disciples (Stephen and James) are actually put to death, and neither of them on a cross. Those in Acts who work to spread the good news suffer rejection, verbal abuse, denunciations, stonings, beatings, jailings, and expulsions. Such is the prophet's fate. When they are rejected in one place they move on to another, but always leaving behind the seeds of a Christian community. Thus Luke structures the plot of Acts to demonstrate that God uses the rejection of these Christian prophets as the prime mechanism for the geographic spread of the gospel.[10]

As for the other side of the disciple paradigm that Johnson finds in the gospels, loving service to others, Luke shows very little interest in it. More than the other evangelists, Luke draws attention to Jesus' compassion and love, primarily through the way he relates Jesus' healings. However, when he narrates the model behavior of the apostles in Acts, we see little of this. Yes, they occasionally heal; but the primary emphasis is on spreading the gospel through preaching, not on selfless love for others.

Tradition and Innovation in the Gospel Patterns

Both Matthew and Luke use Mark's narrative structure as the outline for their own narratives. Both use much more of Mark's content than they omit. So it is not particularly surprising that they both make use of Mark's pattern of Jesus as the suffering Son of Man and of Mark's notion that disciples must be willing to endure persecution. However, Johnson's claim is far stronger than this. He maintains that Matthew and Luke do much more than simply make use of Mark's pattern: he claims that they make it fundamental to their own gospels.

> The Gospels of Matthew and Luke develop the image of Jesus in a distinctive way. Yet each keeps this same fundamental image of Jesus as the suffering Son of man. Each retains the Markan passion account and develops it even further. Each maintains the threefold prediction of the passion. By this means, they place Jesus' ministry of teaching and wonder-working within the framework of rejection and suffering. Something more than respect for a source is at work here. Matthew and Luke feel free to alter virtually every other aspect of Mark, but *this image of the suffering One they do not alter in the least*. Luke and Matthew accept the Markan interpretation of Jesus as religiously true. Their expansions and elaborations confirm rather than suppress this aspect of Jesus' identity. (p. 154, emphasis added)

Johnson's position here is half true. It is true that Matthew and Luke build on Mark's passion narrative and reproduce Mark's passion predictions. It is true that they do not suppress Jesus' suffering.* But the other half of the truth that Johnson does not state is that they both subsume Mark's pattern into their own distinctive ones. The basic point I am arguing is that both Matthew and Luke adapt, supplement, and modify Mark's pattern to such an extent that it is inaccurate and misleading to give the impression that they reaffirm and reinforce Mark's pattern. Johnson creates just this impression and cites a few Matthean and Lukan verses to make it seem plausible. However, the passages and thematic elements Johnson refers to do not represent distinctively Matthean or Lukan configurations of Jesus or discipleship, if these gospels are taken as a whole and understood on their own terms.

Johnson has to work very selectively in order to derive the same pattern from all four gospels. There is nothing objectionable about selectivity per se. It is, in fact, unavoidable and necessary inasmuch as every act of interpretation highlights certain elements of something while ignoring others. Selectivity only becomes a problem when it suppresses contrary evidence or silences countervailing voices. The gospels are built largely out of traditional materials that had lives of their own prior to their inclusion in a gospel. In those previous lives these materials were formulated and held together according to interpretive patterns that the evangelists may or may not agree with or choose to reinforce. The evangelists often make use of traditional material but configure it according to their own patterns, thus endowing it with new and different meanings.†

Evangelists can thus incorporate earlier material without taking over its meaning. Still, some pieces of the earlier patterns remain as unintegrated elements in their new literary settings, which enables us to discern (usually only partially) what meanings these materials had in their earlier lives. This is what makes possible the search for the historical Jesus. It is also what makes it possible for Johnson to find in Matthew and Luke pieces of Mark's pattern. However, Johnson proceeds selectively, locating elements of the

---

* It is not true that Matthew and Luke "do not alter in the least" Mark's "image of the suffering One." A crucial notion in Mark is that Jesus' death was somehow a "ransom" for others, a notion that Luke carefully excises. This is a major alteration. Luke's change of Mark's demand that disciples "carry the cross" to his own requirement that they "carry the cross daily" is also a major modification in the pattern of discipleship.

† An obvious example of this process is how Mark uses traditional material about the disciples and arranges it into an unflattering pattern in which they fail to grasp what Jesus tries to teach them. Matthew was aware of this pattern and systematically altered it to make the disciples into intelligent followers who understand what Jesus teaches.

Markan pattern in Matthew and Luke while not adverting to the abundant evidence that they use Mark's material to create new and distinct patterns. Any biblical scholar allowed the same degree of selectivity that Johnson grants himself could dip into these gospels, come up with a different set of passages, and on this basis describe patterns quite different from the one Johnson finds.

WHAT KIND OF REALITY IS THE "REAL" JESUS?

At the heart of Johnson's rejection of the quest for the historical Jesus is his belief that it cannot sustain religious commitment. He argues that the historical Jesus is an artifact of intellectual labor and so is not a fit object of Christian faith, which is only properly centered on the risen Christ. This distinction, Johnson insists, is "of absolutely fundamental importance."

> Christians direct their faith not to the historical figure of Jesus but to the living Lord Jesus. Yes, they assert continuity between that Jesus and this. But their faith is confirmed, not by the establishment of facts about the past, but by the reality of Christ's power in the present. Christian faith is not directed to a human construction about the past; that would be a form of idolatry. Authentic Christian faith is a response to the living God, whom Christians declare is powerfully at work among them through the resurrected Jesus. (pp. 142–43)

If taken out of the context of Johnson's larger argument, this declaration could seem a flirtation with Docetism. Only the point about the continuity between the risen Jesus and the historical Jesus keeps it from being a denial of his full humanity. If this continuity is to be more than purely formal, it has to include concrete content about the historical Jesus. Commitment to the risen Christ that is not fleshed out with some notion of the specifics of Jesus' historical life would be an evasion of belief in Incarnation. Johnson argues that this content is available neither in the gospel narratives nor in reconstructions of the historical Jesus but in two other sources: the very few facts about Jesus that are beyond any reasonable doubt (primarily that he was a Jew who was crucified around 30 CE) and the gospel pattern that communicates the meaning of his life (a life of obedience to God and love of others).

In Johnson's schema then, belief in the risen Christ entails belief in this pattern. And the truth of this pattern is confirmed in the same way that belief in the risen Christ is confirmed: "not by the establishment of facts about the past,[11] but by the reality of Christ's power in the present" (p. 143).

In the case of a "reality" that allegedly can confirm a belief, it is important that we clarify its ontological status. "The reality of Christ's power in the present" is a reality of religious experience, in the same category as other realities testified to by religious believers, such as the reality of the infinite compassion of the Buddha, the reality of the loving protection of Lord Krishna, the reality of the divine authority of the Qur'an, the reality of the stillness of the Tao, the reality of help from Catholic saints, the reality of Gaia's maternal care, and many other similar realities. When we consider the evidence from Antiquity, nothing allows us to assume that the saving power of deities such as Isis, Asclepius, and Mithras was any less real to those who experienced it than the saving power of Christ was to early Christians.

Christians should have no difficulty recognizing that these other realities are *interpretations* of experiences that are mediated and supported by communities of belief. These interpretations are attempts to name and understand experiences that would otherwise be ineffable.[12] They are, in short, human constructions. If that is true of these other realities, it is difficult to see why it is not also true of the reality Johnson calls "Christ's power in the present." Johnson denies that Christian faith is a response to a human construction; it is rather "a response to the living God whom Christians declare is powerfully at work among them through the resurrected Jesus" (p. 143). This can only mean that for Johnson this Christian declaration is somehow *not* a human interpretation, for if it was, Christian belief "would be a form of idolatry" (p. 143). Johnson thus stakes out a standard position in religious apologetics: the claim that one's beliefs (unlike those of others) are not human interpretations and thus not encumbered by the frailty and fallibility of human knowing; rather, one's beliefs reflect some privileged revelation from God.

Johnson maintains that all four canonical gospels present the life and death of Jesus in exactly the same pattern of meaning. I have argued that when we take the individual gospels on their own terms, no single pattern is evident, but rather an irreducible diversity of patterns.[13] Johnson does not claim that all the gospels say the same thing. He acknowledges the diversity of their narrative presentation of the life and teachings of Jesus.[14] There are several gospel narratives about Jesus because there were several interpretations of his life, death, and teachings. If we recognize that these gospels present the meaning of Jesus' existence in a diversity of patterns, we must likewise acknowledge that these different patterns are themselves intepretations. Since, for Johnson, Christian faith entails belief in the uniform pattern he describes *and* since he asserts that "Christian faith is not directed to a human construction" (p. 143), Johnson cannot allow that the gospel pattern he champions is a human construction. It is therefore crucial for him to argue that the gospels contain only one authoritative pattern, for if we think there is only one pattern, its status as an interpretive artifact is less transparent to us than if we recognize several of them. The thesis that all the canonical sources manifest a single pattern thus makes it easier not to notice that the pattern is an interpretation, that is, a human construction.

Having several patterns forces us to realize that different Christians interpreted the meaning of Jesus in different ways. Having only one pattern leaves undisturbed the uncritical assumption that such a pattern is not an interpretation of Jesus but rather a description of how he really was. This assumption is all the more plausible if one believes that this allegedly sole pattern was based on people's *memories* about Jesus, a claim Johnson reiterates in his analysis of Paul.[15]

The appeal to memory is an appeal to history. And an appeal to history is a powerful claim to authority. The persuasiveness of Johnson's claim to authority depends very much on the impression he creates that the history he appeals to is not some reconstruction based on imperfect evidence, but rather a straightforward and uncomplicated account of what really happened. The final irony in Johnson's apology for what he calls "the classical [Christian] tradition" is that the historical Jesus matters very much to Christian belief, even for someone who claims that he doesn't.

CHAPTER SEVEN

Can the Historical Jesus be Made Safe for Orthodoxy?

A Critique of *The Jesus Quest*

Historical Jesus scholarship has blossomed in the last two decades. So many scholarly studies on the subject have appeared that reading them all has become a formidable professional task. In addition, dozens of books on the historical Jesus have been written for a general audience. The number and variety of these portraits of Jesus have created the need for yet more books that survey the field and sift through the issues for lay readers. One such book, *The Jesus Quest: The Third Search for the Jew from Nazareth* (Downers Grove, Ill.: InterVarsity Press, 1995), by the prolific scholar-author Ben Witherington III, brokers the Jesus debate for conservative Christians and delivers the reassurance that evangelical orthodoxy has nothing to fear from the historical Jesus.

This chapter examines three aspects of Witherington's book: 1) his evaluation of recent historical Jesus scholarship, 2) his position on a central issue relating to the historical Jesus, 3) and his own portrait of the historical Jesus. For (1) I will concentrate on Witherington's critique of *The Five Gospels*. For (2) I will evaluate Witherington's position that Jesus was an apocalyptic figure. This will show how Witherington approaches the problem of establishing the authenticity of specific sayings and how he relates these sayings to Jesus' self-understanding. For (3) I will examine Witherington's portrait of Jesus as incarnate Wisdom.

WITHERINGTON'S CRITIQUE OF THE JESUS SEMINAR

An examination of Witherington's chapter 2 ("Jesus the Talking Head: the Jesus of the Jesus Seminar") can be frustrating because a number of his criticisms seem to be based on misunderstandings. Nevertheless, a careful reading of this chapter can be instructive. It becomes clear that Witherington's disagreements with the the Jesus Seminar are

---

This chapter is slightly revised from its original publication in the *Journal of Higher Criticism* 4 (1997), pp. 120–37. Several of my remarks there are mean-spirited and needlessly divert attention from the real issues. I apologize to Professor Witherington and ask anyone who might quote from or refer to my critique of *The Jesus Quest* to use the more civil version in this chapter.

rooted in his fundamental disagreement with the historical-critical method. While Witherington never makes this disagreement explicit, it is the obvious implication of his assumptions, which are not difficult to detect.

Before analyzing Witherington's criticisms of the Jesus Seminar, we need to address several instances in which he misunderstands or misrepresents it.

- Commenting on the criterion of dissimilarity, he argues that it cannot be used as the "sole determinant of what is authentic among [Jesus'] sayings" (p. 46). Witherington gives no examples of the Seminar using it as the "sole determinant." There are more to be found in *The Five Gospels* because that is not how the Seminar used this criterion.
- Witherington finds a "decided preference" in *The Five Gospels* for Luke's parables (p. 53). He then states, "There is no sound scholarly basis for formulating a general rule that Luke's form of sayings is more likely to be original than Matthew's" (p. 54). The Seminar neither formulated nor used such a rule. Witherington goes on to chide the Seminar: "Each saying must be judged on a case-by-case basis" (p. 54). The Seminar did exactly that, as is abundantly clear from *The Five Gospels*.
- Witherington asserts that "the seminar seems to be overly optimistic not only about the antiquity of the sayings found in the Gospel of Thomas, but also about its independence from the canonical Gospels" (p. 48). He ventures that "of the sayings in Thomas that have no parallels in the synoptics, a *few* may be authentic" (p. 49, emphasis original). Ironically, Witherington is more "optimistic" in this regard than the Seminar, which found no sayings unique to Thomas that it could rate red and only two of them that it could rate pink.
- Witherington chastises the Jesus Seminar for its "omissions" (that is, for "omitting" certain kinds of gospel material from its list of authentic sayings). Among the sayings the Seminar failed to find authentic are "presumably various of the pronouncements in the so-called pronouncement stories" (p. 55). In fact, the Seminar concluded that 40 percent of the pronouncement stories contain authentic pronouncement sayings.* Perhaps this percentage is lower than Witherington expects, but it hardly counts as an "omission."
- Witherington objects that the members of the Seminar "are more confident in *their* reconstruction of Q as representative of the early Jesus tradition than in Mark's presentation of sayings material, even though we have a

---

* There are twenty different pronouncement stories in the gospels, not counting parallels. (For of a list of them, see *The Acts of Jesus*, p. 11.) Of these twenty stories, one contains a pronouncement that is colored red (Mark 12:17) and seven more have pronouncements colored pink (Mark 2:17; 2:19; 2:27–28; Luke (Q) 7:24; 9:58, 60; 11:17–22.

well-established Greek text of Mark, and have no such text for Q" (p. 52). This statement can give the impression that the Seminar used its own reconstruction of Q in its historical investigations. Such an impression would be a mistake. The Seminar did not vote on a reconstructed Q, but on actual sayings in Matthew and Luke.

• Witherington criticizes the Seminar for publishing its work without proper peer review—as if the collaborative work of over seventy qualified scholars needs any more scholars to judge whether it is worthy of being published! Here are his words.

An air of mystery hangs over the seminar's publications. Polebridge Press was set up as the publishing vehicle for the Jesus Seminar, as well as for related projects deemed worthy of publishing by Funk and his editorial board. To my knowledge, the Jesus Seminar has not submitted any of its materials to the scrutiny of established scholars and editors—such as Fortress, Westminster, Eerdmans, Doubleday and Harper, among others—to determine whether this material passes scholarly muster. Rather the material has simply been published by what is in effect the Jesus Seminar's own private publishing company. This should tell us something about how open to critical discussion the Jesus Seminar's working methods and conclusions really are.[1]

In fact, *The Five Gospels* was initially published by Macmillan and then by HarperSanFrancisco, which also published *The Acts of Jesus*.

Witherington also criticizes the Seminar for its voting process, the composition of its membership, and its "not very Jewish" Jesus. I have noted and responded to these in chapter 4 (pp. 65–68 and 74–75). Here I will take up his most substantive disagreement with the Seminar, his criticism of its approach to the critical assessment of the historicity of the gospels. Witherington's objections to it reveal his own understanding of the nature of historical Jesus scholarship.

THE NATURE OF THE CRITICAL STUDY
OF THE HISTORICAL JESUS

In assessing the authenticity of the sayings of Jesus, the Jesus Seminar shouldered a burden of proof: to accept as authentic only those sayings it could demonstrate to be such. This methodological principle is inherent in the critical investigation of the historicity of the gospels. The gospels were written decades after Jesus by people who worshiped him as a divine being and regarded him as the spokesman for their own beliefs and ideals. Texts with such a blatant bias make no claim to be objective reporting, and no critical historian would think of simply assuming they were. This is plain common sense: historians should treat textual material as historical evidence only if they can establish its historicity.

Witherington does not directly address the issue of the burden of proof, but his perspective is discernible in his criticism of the Seminar's use of a critical standard in assessing the historicity of the gospels. He objects to the

apparent presumption of many members of the seminar that sayings *must* be regarded as inauthentic unless they are proven to be authentic.[2] This is assumed to be *the* critical point of view. But in reality it is a perspective steeped in a negative bias, not a neutral or open stance (p. 47, emphasis original).

It seems that for Witherington a neutral stance is one that suspends critical judgment and takes an ancient writer's word at face value. This seems to be the moral of the following statement:

Too often scholars . . . assume they know better than the early Christians who preserved and collected the sayings of Jesus and composed the Gospels what Jesus was or was not likely to have said. This assumption is founded on hubris (p. 48).

This makes it clear that Witherington is opposed not only to the specific methods of the Jesus Seminar, but to the historical-critical method in general. And Witherington's verdict on the historical-critical method is that it is founded on hubris. Rather than accepting the need for a critical sifting of the evidence, Witherington calls on us to submit to the authority of the canonical gospels and defer to their judgment about what Jesus said. Of course, this overlooks the problem of which evangelist to trust, since they often give quite different versions of Jesus' sayings. It also ignores the fact that Matthew and Luke deliberately modify sayings they find in Mark and Q. Matthew and Luke apparently assumed *they* knew better than Christians before them what Jesus had said. On Witherington's logic, then, the gospels of Matthew and Luke are themselves products of hubris.

The most unusual of Witherington's criticisms of the Jesus Seminar is one that reveals his own (mis)understanding of the very basis for historical Jesus research. In criticizing the composition of the Seminar, Witherington complains that none of its members are fundamentalists. He states that fundamentalists could not participate in the Seminar because its approach is biased to present a non-fundamentalist portrait of the historical Jesus (p. 44).* The

---

* Actually, fundamentalists could join the Seminar if they wished, but Witherington is correct to think they would feel out of place.

absence of fundamentalists from the Jesus Seminar can be construed as a sign of bias in its agenda *only on the assumption that historical Jesus research can be conducted on the basis of fundamentalist convictions.* But obviously, if we start with the belief in the literal historicity of every verse in the Bible, we rule out, by definition, critical judgments about the historical reliability of anything in the gospels. Witherington's assumption here that an unbiased approach to the historical Jesus must include the fundamentalist perspective really amounts to a rejection of the very basis of historical-critical scholarship.

For Witherington, apparently, the quest for the historical Jesus does not involve questioning the historical reliability of the gospel material, but consists of fitting it all into a harmonized composite. Consider one of his closing comments on the Jesus Seminar. Referring to the Seminar's conclusion that 18% of the sayings can confidently be traced to the historical Jesus, Witherington objects that

> [the Seminar] rejects the majority of the evidence (82%) . . . I will leave the reader to decide whether it is a truly scholarly and unbiased approach to reject the majority of one's evidence and stress a minority of it (p. 57).

This statement implies that Witherington accepts *all* the gospel material to be evidence for the historical Jesus; *only* on this assumption could he accuse the Seminar of "rejecting" evidence. Without this assumption, one could not say that the Seminar rejects any evidence for the historical Jesus, but rather that it finds only 18% of the sayings to *be* evidence for the historical Jesus. This is not "rejecting" evidence; it is making judgments about what kind of evidence each saying is: some sayings are evidence for the teachings of the historical Jesus and some are evidence for the beliefs of early Christians who attributed their own words to Jesus.

Witherington concludes his chapter on the Jesus Seminar with a sweeping dismissal of its work. What is interesting are the reasons Witherington gives for why he believes the Jesus of the Jesus Seminar is not credible historically: "this seminar Jesus will not preach" and "did not come to save" (p. 57). Witherington's assurance this "this seminar Jesus" cannot be the object of contemporary Christian preaching seems to imply that since Witherington cannot preach this Jesus, no Christian could or should. In fact, numerous pastors have responded enthusiastically to the public work of the Seminar because this Jesus is one they *can* preach. Apart from that, however, Witherington's verdict on the Jesus Seminar shows clearly that his standards for historical research on Jesus are not historical at all, but theological.

Witherington's bottom line for the historical Jesus is that Witherington be able to preach him and that he be the bringer of "salvation" in the distinctive sense that Witherington's theological tradition understands it.

JESUS AND APOCALYPTIC

Witherington maintains that the historical Jesus was an apocalyptic preacher, but an exceptionally odd one: one who wasn't sure whether the End was imminent. According to Witherington, Jesus preached that the End *might* be coming soon. Furthermore, this Jesus understood himself in terms of the Son of Man in Daniel 7, who, apparently, might or might not be coming soon. Witherington builds his argument on three legs.

The first leg of Witherington's case is that the gospel sayings about the future Son of Man all come from the historical Jesus. He offers three reasons for this position: 1) they meet the criterion of double dissimilarity; 2) they are presupposed in the sayings where the Son of Man is a present figure; 3) there is multiple independent attestation for this kind of saying.

1. Witherington argues that the future Son of Man sayings meet the criterion of dissimilarity because (a) there was no Jewish expectation of a coming of the Son of Man, and because (b) the coming Son of Man was not part of early Christian theology. The first claim denies what the most famous Son of Man text in the Old Testament (Dan 7:13) explicitly describes: "one like a son of man coming with the clouds of heaven." We are told, however, that Daniel 7 "seems to speak of a Son of Man going up into the presence of God, not of a Son of Man coming down to earth" (p. 97). On Witherington's own terms, then, it seems that Jesus misunderstood Daniel 7.

As for (1b), Witherington's claim that the coming Son of Man is not part of early Christian theology is based on the fact that this concept is not found outside the gospels. This assumes that the gospels are not evidence for what early Christians believed. As odd as that assumption will seem to readers familiar with the critical study of the gospels, it is a cornerstone of Witherington's approach, because for him the gospels are evidence for what the historical Jesus said and thought and did, not for early Christian interpretations of Jesus. Witherington either doesn't realize or doesn't care that this begs the entire question of the historical Jesus. It coheres perfectly with his assumption that the quest for the historical Jesus is compatible with Fundamentalism (see above).

2. A problem in understanding Son of Man terminology is that the gospels use it not only to refer to a future apocalyptic figure, but also as Jesus' self-

designation in the here-and-now of the narrative. So if Jesus saw the Son of Man as one who will act in the future, how could he describe his own activity as that of the Son of Man? Witherington explains,

> [Jesus] saw God's eschatological activity already occurring in and through his ministry . . . Thus even in the "present" Son of Man sayings, the context of Daniel 7 stands in the background (p. 95).

Forget about the plain sense of the texts: even when Jesus is talking about the present he's thinking about the future.

3. Contrary to Witherington, an obstacle to tracing the future Son of Man sayings to the historical Jesus is that they are not multiply attested. Some occur in Mark and some in Q, but none of the sayings are attested in two independent sources. Witherington sidesteps this problem by taking the sayings as a group: the future Son of Man sayings "as a *general* category meet the criterion of multiple attestation" (p. 96, emphasis original). It's hard to know what to make of this. Apparently, Witherington believes that although the sayings themselves are not mutliply attested, they should be taken as authentic because the general category is. One repeatedly gets the impression that Witherington is not out to determine which sayings or deeds go back to Jesus. To his mind, they all do. His only real challenge is to find the arguments that point to this preordained conclusion. And since he obviously writes for those who believe as he does (for who else would be persuaded by his arguments except for those who share his assumptions?), any argument will do.

The second leg of Witherington's case for the apocalyptic Jesus takes us into strange territory. It starts with Witherington's consideration of Mark 13:32: "As for the exact day or hour, no one knows, not even the angels in heaven, nor even the son, no one, except the Father." Although this saying is not attested independently of Mark, Witherington believes it is authentic. His reason: "It is quite unbelievable that the early church would have fabricated this" (p. 96).* Unbelievable to Witherington, perhaps, but for others it is quite believable that early Christians might well have invented this saying as a way of explaining why Jesus had not been more precise in his predictions, or as a way of taking out insurance on his credibility, just in case the End proved tardy. Be that as it may, Witherington's conclusion is stunning:

---

* Witherington seems unwilling to acknowledge that the early church would have fabricated *any* saying of Jesus.

[Mark 13:32] can only mean one thing: Jesus did not proclaim that the end was *necessarily* imminent. At most he could only have spoken of its possible imminence, something which I believe he did do (p. 96, emphasis original).

Jesus' message, then, was: "the End is near, maybe." A serious problem for Witherington's thesis is that, just two verses before 13:32, Mark reports that Jesus unequivocally announced that the End *was* imminent: "Truly I tell you, this generation will not pass away until all these things have taken place" (Mark 13:30—where "all these things" includes the coming of the Son of Man.) Witherington doesn't address this muddle here, though in passing references to Mark 13:30 elsewhere (pp. 100, 133, 210), he asserts that this saying refers to the end of the temple, not to the End itself. He gives no reason why we should believe that 13:30 refers only to the end of the temple, while 13:32 refers to the End of the cosmos. There are no grounds whatsoever in Mark's context to distinguish what Jesus is talking about in 13:30 from what he is talking about in 13:32.

Witherington's problems are generated by his commitment to the historical truth of the gospels. Since for him the gospel tradition all comes from Jesus, the only real challenge is to figure out how all the pieces can fit together into a coherent mosaic. A big problem is that the gospel material can be stubbornly inconsistent with itself. Considerable ingenuity is needed to explain away such inconsistencies, especially in cases (like this one) that require the harmonizer to ignore or contradict the clear meaning of the text. Critical scholars who are not intent on harmonization take these mismatches as evidence that the words and deeds of Jesus were given new meanings by early Christians or that early Christians differed among themselves over the meaning of Jesus' words, deeds, and identity. But for Witherington all the gospel material is evidence for the historical Jesus.

Although Witherington's premises are flawed, his logic is valid. If Mark 13:32 (which refers to the End) comes from Jesus, it follows that he could not have proclaimed with confidence that the End was near (even though he does in 13:30). Elsewhere Jesus speaks of the End and the coming of the Son of Man without such reticence, but since 13:32 has to fit into the mosaic, Witherington has to imagine Jesus crossing his fingers as he preached: even when he says the End is near, he only means it *might* be near. Unfortunately, Jesus was unable to convey this nuance effectively, because just a few years after this death, some of his followers were anticipating the End within their own lifetimes. Witherington explains that the future Son of Man sayings led "some Christians to the erroneous conclusion that Jesus had spoken of a necessarily imminent end" (p. 97).

The conclusion that some early Christians misunderstood or deliberately changed what Jesus meant is not unusual among critical scholars. Tracing out the modulations in the meaning of sayings as they function in Jesus' own context, in the context of this or that Christian preachment, and in the literary contexts of the gospels is a traditional cottage industry in New Testament scholarship. That different sectors of the Jesus movement reinterpreted (or misinterpreted) the teaching of the master (for example, by making the parables refer to Jesus himself) is a standard working hypothesis. However, it is surprising for Witherington to take this position: earlier in his book when he criticized the Jesus Seminar, he protested that it was an act of "hubris" for modern scholars to think that they understand Jesus better than his ancient followers.

The third facet of Witherington's discussion of Jesus and apocalyptic has to do with Jesus' self-understanding. Not only did Jesus predict the (possibly) imminent coming of the Son of Man, he believed that he himself was that Son of Man. According to Witherington, Jesus recognized himself in the apocalyptic scenario of Daniel: "the Daniel 7 material was foundational for Jesus' understanding of who he was and what God wished him to do and proclaim" (p. 97). Witherington does not say how he knows this, nor does he so much as advert to the methodological leaps entailed in claiming to know such a precise detail of someone's psychology without autobiographical evidence. For the sake of argument, however, let's grant Witherington his assertion and notice what it entails.

First, it entails a curious lacuna in Jesus' self-knowledge: according to Witherington, Jesus knew he was the Son of Man who was going to return to earth on the clouds, but he didn't know when he would return. Second, it means that Jesus' self-understanding was based on a *mistake*. Daniel 7 does not portray the "one like a son of man" as an individual human being; it presents this figure as a symbol for the whole people of Israel, just as the horrific beasts that precede it represent conquering kingdoms. This is not a modern exegetical opinion; this is how Daniel 7 itself explicitly interprets its own symbolism (see Dan 7:17–18, 23–27). Witherington maintains that when Jesus read Daniel 7 he believed that he was reading about himself. For Jesus to think that the one like a son of man could be an individual person (that is, Jesus himself) would be to misinterpret Daniel 7. That is not Jesus' only mistake, however. According to Witherington, the Son of Man in Daniel 7 does not come to earth on the clouds, but rather goes up to God on them. Yet if one takes Mark 13:26 as an authentic saying (as Witherington does), Jesus understands the Son of Man to ride the clouds from heaven to earth. In short, Witherington's Jesus comes to his self-understanding with a combination of ignorance and error.

That Jesus made mistakes and didn't know some important things is, obviously, not a problem for historians nor for Christians who believe in Jesus' full humanity. However, as we will see, Witherington maintains that the historical Jesus, in addition to being the coming Son of Man, was also the incarnation of divine Wisdom. For incarnate Wisdom to manifest such ignorance and error about his self-understanding is, to say the least, incongruous and unseemly.

WISDOM INCARNATE

In *The Jesus Quest* Witherington analyzes the works of some twenty scholars, treating his own previous work within this format. We thus have Witherington's own summary of his views on Jesus, entitled "Jesus the Sage, the Embodiment of Wisdom" (pp. 185–96). Witherington begins by pointing out that Jesus' primary mode of discourse is in wisdom genres (riddles, parables, aphorisms, etc.). That Jesus was a teacher in the wisdom tradition is non-controversial. According to Witherington, however, Jesus not only taught wisdom; he was Wisdom itself.

Witherington makes his case by reading several of Jesus' sayings as indirect self-references. According to Witherington:

- When Jesus said, "Wisdom is vindicated by her deeds" (Matt 11:19), he was referring to himself. Witherington argues that some of the deeds that vindicate Jesus as Wisdom are his meals with outcasts, which show that Jesus was acting out the part of Wisdom holding a feast for unlikely guests (p. 187).
- In the "foxes have holes" saying (Q 9:58), Jesus articulates his own experience "in light of what happened to Wisdom according to the late wisdom material in 1 Enoch 42" (p. 188). Witherington claims that another text that influenced Jesus' formulation of this saying was Sir 36:31 ("Who will trust a man that has no nest, but lodges wherever night overtakes him?"). Witherington overlooks or ignores the fact that Sirach here is critical of the itinerant.
- In the lament over Jerusalem (Q 13:34–35), "Jesus saw his rejection by Jerusalem as the rejection of God's Wisdom" (p. 188).
- Q 10:21–22 ("No one knows who the son is except the Father, or who the Father is except the son") expresses Jesus' relationship to God in terms that resemble Wisdom's relationship to God. In addition, "Jesus' use of *abba* indicates that he believed he had a unique relationship to God"

(p. 189). Witherington does not explain how this squares with Jesus' instruction for all to address God as father (Q 11:2) or his inclusive use of the term "sons of God" (for example, Q 6:35, Matt 5:9).

- When Jesus quotes Wisdom ("The Wisdom of God said . . .") in Luke 11:49, he "may have identified himself directly as God's Wisdom" (p. 189).

In discussing these five sayings, Witherington gives a one-sentence argument for the authenticity of Q 10:21–22, and no argument whatever either for the authenticity of the other four sayings or for his assertion that in these sayings Jesus portrayed himself as Wisdom. It's not as if Witherington is unaware of the need for arguments. In his discussion of Luke 11:49 and Matt 11:19 he explains that these sayings would confirm his view that Jesus saw himself as Wisdom if their authenticity could be demonstrated. However, Witherington does not claim to have demonstrated this, only that "the arguments I advanced . . . go some distance toward validating their authenticity" (p. 189). This uncommon reticence is mooted, however, by the fact that the "arguments" Witherington refers to are bare assertions and not arguments at all. But no matter: his "case does not need to rest solely on such explicit statements" (p. 189).

Witherington then goes on to explain how numerous Jesus sayings are sapiential in form, content, and style (pp. 189–90). He offers no arguments at all for the historicity of any of these sayings. But, what is more bewildering, he seems to think that Jesus' traffic in sapiential material somehow supports the conclusion that Jesus saw himself as Wisdom incarnate.

Witherington does not think that Jesus' self-understandinging was innate. It was something Jesus had to discover and Witherington believes that he knows how Jesus did it.

> [Sirach 24] sees Torah as the locus where wisdom exists on earth . . . It was not a far step from this to identifying a particular person instead of a thing with God's Wisdom . . . Jesus took this step, in concert with his belief that he was God's divine agent, God's apostle or sent one, endowed with a divine. commission, an intimate knowledge of the Sender's mind and purposes (p. 192).

Jesus may have found additional support for this self-understanding in other texts.

> Jesus may have seen the Wisdom hymn of Proverbs 8 or Sirach 24, even Wisdom of Solomon 8–9, as the clue to his own career and its outcome (p. 193).

This kind of reasoning is typical of Witherington's writing. If he can see a connection, he asserts it as if it were obvious to all, either unaware or unconcerned about how others may look at it. His claim that "it was not a far step" from believing Torah to be the locus of wisdom to identifying a particular person as Wisdom in the flesh is a perfect example. Torah was the word of God, the holiest and most precious object in Jewish life, revered for centuries. It therefore is simply audacious to suggest that believing Torah to be the locus of wisdom is almost the same as thinking that an itinerant carpenter from an obscure village is Wisdom incarnate. If that weren't enough, a few pages later Witherington suggests that Wisdom incarnate, who has "an intimate knowledge of [God's] mind," had to read wisdom literature to pick up clues about his own career!

For the sake of the argument, let us assume that Witherington is correct and Jesus truly did believe he was Wisdom incarnate. If Jesus was right about himself, what does that entail? For one thing, it entails that the personification of Wisdom in the late wisdom literature is not simply a literary device and the story of Wisdom is not a myth. It is a metaphysical reality. It turns out that there actually was a supernatural being named Wisdom, a being distinct from God that came to earth in human form.

Two questions arise. 1) Theologically, how can this be reconciled with the doctrine of the Trinity, according to which Jesus is the incarnation of the Son? 2) If Jesus was Wisdom incarnate, and knew that he was, why did he not say so directly and clearly? Why is Wisdom so coy and indirect about identifying himself (or herself)? Early Christians identified Jesus as Messiah, son of God, son of Man, and Logos, but never as Wisdom. It seems, then, that Wisdom incarnate was unsuccessful in communicating the truth about himself to his own followers.

In Witherington's view, Jesus believed himself to be something more than a human being. He goes so far as to assert that Jesus understood himself to be a *divine* being ("God's divine agent"), Wisdom personified. At the end of one of his earlier books, Witherington posed the question: "Did Jesus think himself to be divine?"[3] Witherington answered that Jesus did not use the word "God" for himself; that is Christian language. However, Witherington speculated that if Jesus could have read the Gospel of John, "he would have found that Gospel a suitable expression of his identity"[4]. Remember that in the climactic scene in John's gospel the disciple Thomas doubts that Jesus had been raised from from the dead. When Thomas sees him in person, however, he falls to his knees and addresses him as "my God" (John 20:28). Witherington, then, believes that Jesus would have agreed with Thomas that he was God. Since Witherington insists (rightly) that the historical Jesus must be understood squarely within the context of Judaism, the "God" whom Jesus believed himself to be can only have been Judaism's God, none other than Yahweh himself, the creator of the universe. How could a Jew believe this about himself? How could this thought even arise in a sane Jewish mind?

Such a farfetched claim about the historical Jesus makes the apologetical purpose of Witherington's scholarship transparent. It also reveals Witherington's understanding of the task of biblical scholarship, namely, to provide exegetical cover for the truth of his own theological tradition. Witherington's position that Jesus thought he was a divine being puts him on the extreme right wing of historical Jesus scholars. However, in my view, this is not the strangest position Witherington takes. Once he combines his view of who Jesus believed himself to be (Wisdom incarnate) with his view of the nature of Jesus' apocalyptic message (that the End was possibly imminent), Witherington gets a Jesus who is self-consciously divine Wisdom (with "an intimate knowledge of [God's] mind and purpose") and whose message to humanity was that the End of the world *might* be coming soon. What stops me here is not so much the sheer implausibility of this christological scenario, but the triviality of what divine Wisdom has to say. "The End might be coming soon" is a statement that is equally true at every moment in history, logically equivalent to statements such as "next month you might get a raise." Statements like this are always true because no subsequent state of affairs can possibly prove them wrong. In the nomenclature of contemporary philosophy, such statements are "trivially true" because they tell us (literally) nothing about the world. If Witherington is right that this was indeed at the center of Jesus' message, then Jesus had nothing important to say.

WITHERINGTON'S AUDIENCE

Witherington shows (to his own satisfaction) that rigorous scholarship (as he construes it) can establish that the historical Jesus believed himself to be a pre-existent divine being come to earth. It will be obvious to all who read Witherington that he does not believe that Jesus was wrong. One way to see Witherington's book, then, is as a kind of gospel, inasmuch as its message is intended to be good news. It is useful, then, to ask a question that we routinely ask about the ancient gospels: who is its implied audience? That is, who would be persuaded by Witherington's case that Jesus proclaimed himself to be Wisdom incarnate, and for whom would this be good news?

My hunch is that the only readers who will concur with Witherington that Jesus believed himself to be the incarnation of a divine being are those who start his book with this conviction. Those for whom this is "good news" are those who believe, not only that Jesus saw himself this way, but that Jesus was right about himself. Witherington's implied audience, then, are Christians who believe that Jesus is God and who also want to believe that biblical scholarship can demonstrate that the historical Jesus believed this about himself.

While most Christians traditionally have believed that Jesus is divine, it has only been in the last few years that the need has arisen for assurance from biblical scholars that the historical Jesus shared this belief. Why so? Because only recently have traditional believers been disturbed by biblical scholarship that emphasizes the difference between the Jesus of history and the Christ of faith. Biblical scholars have long questioned (or denied) the historical reliability of the gospels, but only in the last decade or so have some of them communicated this directly and without equivocation to the American public. Previously, fundamentalists enjoyed a virtual monopoly over public discourse on the Bible, with the likes of Pat Robertson and Jerry Falwell being the only "experts" on the Bible in the public eye.

In recent years traditional believers have become aware of television documentaries about Jesus (such as those in the series "Mysteries of the Bible") and best-selling books, along with the talk show and press interviews with their authors, in which a professor of New Testament (or even a bishop) has told the American public that the historical Jesus was a far different figure than the one portrayed in the canonical gospels. All this cannot but be disturbing to many conservative Christians. Although these troublemaking scholars have been denounced from the pulpit, this no longer seems quite enough. What is needed are champions of the faith who can defend orthodoxy from within the scholarly guild.

Witherington's book fills this bill exactly: he analyzes all the important new books on Jesus, commends them when they support orthodox views, exposes their deficiencies and errors when they do not, and proposes his own historical Jesus that is perfectly compatible with evangelical theology. In short, Witherington delivers the goods for orthodoxy. He writes to reassure those troubled by the likes of Borg, Crossan, or Funk and their notorious fellow travelers in the Jesus Seminar. According to Witherington, these scholars have misread the texts, ignored the evidence, and made judgments based on prejudice or ideology. So not only are these skeptics wrong religiously in that they deny the Christian faith, they are wrong intellectually and thus have failed as scholars.

Readers outside of Witherington's implied audience will detect a certain irony in the "quest" and "search" terminology of the title of his book. There is no real doubt about where Witherington's "quest" will end because this quest is not one to discover who the historical Jesus was. For Witherington (and for other scholar-apologists who share his approach) this is determined, not by historical research, but by theological affirmation: the historical Jesus is the divine figure of traditional Christian belief. The search is not for the correct understanding of Jesus because this was never lost; it was there all along in the creed.

Yet there is a quest in *The Jesus Quest*: the quest for scholarly support for a historical Jesus who is also the Christ of the creeds. This quest knows where it has to end up; the only question is how to get there. This apologetical quest, whatever its merits, is not a *critical* enterprise. Indeed its purpose is the very opposite. For Witherington's audience the success of this quest is judged not by the cogency of its argument, but by the orthodoxy of its results.

CHAPTER EIGHT

Apologetics and the Resurrection

Anyone interested in the historical Jesus sooner or later must come to terms with the resurrection stories. The question we have to face is of whether it can be demonstrated historically that Jesus rose from the dead. Regardless of how we might answer that question, all of us today understand what it is asking. But for nearly all of Christian history the question itself would have made no sense. Christians believed in the resurrection because the Church taught it as a truth of the Faith. Jesus' resurrection did not need to be demonstrated. Those inside the Church believed it because the Bible said so and the Bible was universally believed to be literally and historically true. Believing this took no special effort because there was no reason to think otherwise. Those who did not believe that Jesus had risen from the dead were outside the Church (they were Jews for the most part), and so were regarded as willfully rejecting God's truth. Insiders did not need any proof of the central truths of the Christian faith. As for outsiders, there was no point in trying.

For most Christians in today's world, belief in the resurrection works the way it always has. They believe that Jesus rose because it says so in the Bible. Case closed. However, belief in the literal truth of the Bible is no longer universal among Christians. There are some Christians whose belief in the resurrection has been shaken by doubts about the historical truth of the Bible. Also, many Christians accept the Bible as God's word but do not believe it is always literally true. Some of these Christians believe in the resurrection but do not take the Easter stories literally. Furthermore, a growing number of Christians are willing to learn about other people's religions. The more they learn, the less credible it seems to these Christians that those in other religions who do not believe in Jesus' resurrection are the enemies of God who have turned their backs on the truth.

For those who are not convinced that every passage in the Bible is literally true, the question naturally arises whether the resurrection stories in the gospels are historically accurate. Those who believe that the resurrection is literally true and who want to persuade others of that belief cannot simply

This chapter is adapted from "What Do Stories About Resurrection(s) Prove?" in *Will the Real Jesus Please Stand Up?* edited by Paul Copan (Grand Rapids: Baker Books, 1998), pp. 77–98.

appeal to the authority of the Bible. Those who wonder about the historical accuracy of a set of gospel stories will not have their questions answered by being told that the Bible is the word of God. These people are asking a historical question and it won't do to give them religious assurances or to exhort them to have faith. They need good historical reasons to believe that Jesus literally rose from the dead. What is needed, then, is an *apology* for the resurrection.*

Christian apologetics is the attempt to prove that the beliefs of Christianity are reasonable. It has a long and venerable history and today is cultivated especially among evangelical Christians, who emphasize the need to spread their Christian faith to everyone. Christian apologetics fits in perfectly with the evangelical mission to "make disciples of all nations" (see Matt 28:20), because its aim is to show that Christian beliefs are in harmony with human reason.

There are many evangelical apologies for Jesus' resurrection in print.[1] Their central thesis is that the literal, bodily resurrection of Jesus is a historical fact that can be proven by solid evidence and sound reasoning. Evangelical apologetics is confident that the evidence for the historical reliability of the gospels is so clear and compelling that those who approach the matter with good will and an open mind will conclude that the gospels are historically accurate records of the words and deeds of Jesus. Evangelical apologies for the resurrection often convey the impression that you don't actually need religious faith to affirm Jesus' literal resurrection; you need only think clearly and objectively about the evidence and draw unbiased conclusions.

It is not my aim here to respond directly to the arguments in these apologies. Rather, I want to step back from them and analyze their general format, message, and audience. I take this approach because their message about the resurrection and the way they communicate that message to their audience is similar in some important ways to the message of the gospels and the way they convey it to their audience. For this reason, understanding the method and message of evangelical apologetics for the resurrection can help to clarify our understanding of the meaning of the resurrection stories in the gospels.

First I will analyze the apologetic attempt to persuade us that Jesus' resurrection is a historical fact. I pay special attention to how and for whom this kind of persuasion succeeds. Then I will use these insights to analyze the res-

---

* The term "apology" here has nothing to do with saying you're sorry. In the sense the term has here, an apology is a rational defense for a certain belief. Hence an apology for the resurrection is an argument that it is reasonable to believe that Jesus was raised from the dead.

urrection stories in the Gospel of Matthew. My aim is to discern what Matthew thought he was doing in telling those stories in just the way he did and how his audience understood them.

APOLOGETICS AND OUTSIDERS

Apologies exist only because there are people who reject, doubt, or simply do not share a given belief. An apology for a belief is essentially a response to whatever casts doubt on it or questions its truth. The root meaning of the word "apology" is "defense," and something can be defended only if it is, or is perceived to be, under attack.[2] A good amount of apologetics is intended to refute the thinking of those who challenge the truth of the belief being defended. By its very nature, apologetics presupposes a context in which there are insiders and outsiders (for example, those who share the belief being defended and those who do not).

Apologetics is thus unavoidably adversarial. This doesn't mean that apologies have to be belligerent or mean-spirited, though some certainly are. It simply means that apologies always presuppose opponents. It is only natural, then, that apologies generally seem to be addressed to outsiders. They look like attempts to persuade others to change their minds and adopt new beliefs. But is this impression accurate? Are apologies really meant for outsiders? This is a crucial question. The way we answer it helps to shape our perspective on another issue: how we approach the vital question of the historical accuracy of the gospel stories.

Who is the real audience for apologies? One way to determine this is to refocus the question, asking not who seems to be the intended audience, but asking instead who actually reads apologies. Start with yourself.

How often do *you* read material that tries to persuade you that your religious beliefs are wrong and that other beliefs you reject are true? Unless you are yourself an apologist scouting the opposition, the chances are that you've never studied an apology to which you were an outsider. If apologies are actually intended for outsiders, they have to judged colossal failures.

In the few cases when outsiders do read or listen to apologies, they seldom take them seriously (for example, in the spirit in which they present themselves). Outsiders approach apologies with caution, for the simple reason that apologies ask them to change their beliefs. Most outsiders assume that apologies are strongly biased, that they tell only one side of the story. The very few outsiders who read apologies almost always do so out of curiosity, or out of a desire to figure out how to refute them. It is exceedingly rare for outsiders to approach an apology with a willingness to give up their own beliefs.* (You can check this by asking yourself if you were to read literature from the Hare Krishna movement, how seriously you would open your heart and mind to the possibility that Krishna is the Supreme Lord of the Universe.)

We can get a feel for how outsiders regard apologetics by briefly considering an apology for a religion other than Christianity.

AN APOLOGY FOR ISLAM

Islam is an important religion for Christians to consider because Muslims and Christians worship the same God, the one true God who spoke to Abraham, gave the commandments to Moses, and anointed Jesus to be Messiah.† Both religions have very similar understandings of their own beginnings. Islam and Christianity both claim that they originated through the direct intervention of God, through a divine miracle that is unparalleled and unsurpassable. Both believe that God had intervened at various times in the past to reveal His will for humanity, but that those revelations were provisional and incomplete. Both believe that God finally intervened with a perfect revelation that gives us everything we need to know to do His will and find salvation. For Christians, this miracle of perfect revelation is the life, death, and resurrection of Jesus. For Muslims, this miracle is the Qur'an revealed through the prophet Muhammad.

Muslim apologists maintain that unbiased consideration of the evidence confirms the belief that Islam was established by God through the miracle of the Qur'an. Although this miracle was not in itself public (there was nothing to see), reason can nonetheless confirm it by assessing its effects. That is, the divine origin of the Qur'an is the only rational explanation for a number of otherwise inexplicable realities.

First, the Qur'an is completely inerrant. It contains no contradictions and no errors of any kind, not even scientific ones. In fact, some of its descriptions of natural phenomena are consistent with scientific discoveries made centuries after Muhammad.[3]

Second, the Qur'an is unsurpassed in the beauty of its poetry and the

---

* Outsiders assume (correctly) that the apologist is not willing to give up *his* beliefs. Outsiders thus suspect (again correctly) that the apologist is, in effect, saying to them, "I'm asking you to be more open-minded than I am," even if an apologist would never be so crude in his actual wording.

† The Muslim name for God, "*Allah*," is simply the Arabic word "God." Jews and Christians who speak Arabic also refer to God as *Allah*.

grandeur of its language (which can be fully appreciated only in Arabic). The Qur'an even challenges those who do not believe in its divine origin to create a chapter, or even one verse, that compares with it. The Qur'an is a literary masterpiece, yet Muhammad was uneducated and illiterate.

Third, the Qur'an has great spiritual power. It had a profound effect on those who heard it, moving them deeply and leading many to convert to Islam the first time they heard it.

Fourth, the Qur'an's sublime monotheism and its elevated moral teaching were far ahead of the time and place of its earthly origin. Seventh-century Arabia was a place of deeply rooted polytheism and rampant violence, widespread vice, and harsh social oppression. The Qur'an's uncompromising monotheism and its demand for social justice and strict personal morality were utterly foreign to its environment.

Finally, Muhammad never wavered in his claim that the Qur'an was from God and not from him. This claim reflects his sincere belief, for Muhammad was neither a liar nor a megalomaniac nor delusional. He was famous for his honesty; even his enemies admired his integrity. Far from being a megalomaniac, his lifestyle was modest and unassuming and he drew a strict distinction between the times when he was relaying revelation and the times when he was expressing his own thoughts. Neither was Muhammad delusional. His enormous successes as a social reformer and as a political and military leader amply demonstrate his keen grasp of reality.

Further evidence for the divine origin of Islam is the speed at which it grew in a time and place that were hostile to it. Nothing in the culture of seventh-century Arabia favored Islam's monotheism or its elevated and demanding morality. In fact, there were powerful religious, economic, social, and political forces arrayed against it. Muhammad's first followers in Mecca were cruelly persecuted and his fledgling community in Medina was attacked by vastly superior military forces. Islam not only survived, but spread so rapidly that by the time of Muhammad's death just two years after his return to Mecca, virtually all of Arabia had embraced Islam.

Please bear in mind that all this is merely the rough sketch of an apology for Islam. A Muslim scholar of Islam (I am neither) could present these ideas and others with much more force and eloquence. Yet even if this apology were laid out with far greater knowledge and skill than I can manage, how convincing do you think it would be to Christians? How many Christians would it convince that Islam is the religion God intends for all humanity? If you are not a Muslim, how seriously does it make you question your beliefs?

Muslim apologists maintain that the Qur'an would not be so inerrant, profound, beautiful, and compelling if God were not its Author, and that

Islam would not have been accepted by so many so quickly unless it were divinely guided. Muslims find this line of argument quite convincing. Non-Muslims, however, will not be persuaded, even if they do not know how to explain the admirable qualities of the Qur'an or the impressive growth of early Islam. They will assume that even if they themselves do not know how to refute the apology, there are experts who do.

Outsiders seldom read apologies and seldom take them seriously when they do. As for the few who do read an apology and give it serious consideration, how many are actually persuaded by it? Again the answer is: very, very few, if any at all.[4]

THE RESURRECTION FROM THE OUTSIDE

Having seen how an apology for some other religion looks to us (for the sake of the argument I am assuming that you are Christian), we can round out the process with a "thought experiment." Imagine that you are not a Christian, but that you've come across an apology for the literal historicity of Jesus' resurrection. For whatever reason, you take it seriously and decide to make a careful study of the relevant gospel stories. As you read the stories about the empty tomb and the appearances of the risen Jesus, you notice again and again how different they are from gospel to gospel. So you construct charts that lay out the similarities and the differences (see the three charts below).

The four stories about the discovery of the empty tomb are clearly accounts of the same event. It's not as if these are stories about four different visits to the tomb. So it's obvious that these four stories cannot all be literally true. On the other hand, the stories about the appearances of Jesus all seem to be about different encounters (except for Luke 24:36–51 and John 20:19–23, which might be different versions of the same scene). The differences among the appearance stories are therefore not matters of inconsistency or contradiction as in the empty tomb stories. But they do raise the question of why different gospels tell such different stories (again noting the one possible overlap between Luke and John). Isn't it curious that each of them relates completely different appearances?

So, what do you make of all the disparities in the stories. (Remember that for the sake of this thought experiment you are not a Christian and that you are studying these stories for the first time.) Perhaps you conclude that the early Christians couldn't keep their stories straight, or that nobody knew what had actually happened. Maybe at one time somebody did, but by the

CHART ONE
Empty Tomb Stories

	Mark	Matthew	Luke	John
when?	sunrise	before dawn	daybreak	still dark
who?	Mary Magdalene, Mary James' mother, Salome	Mary Magdalene, the other Mary	Mary Magdalene, Mary James' mother, Joanna, other women	Mary Magdalene
condition of tomb	stone already rolled away	angel rolls stone away during earthquake	stone already rolled away	stone already rolled away
guards present?	no	yes	no	no
figure at/in tomb	young man sitting inside tomb	angel sitting on stone outside tomb	no one at first, then two men appear	two angels sitting inside tomb
message	tell the disciples to go to Galilee	tell the disciples to go to Galilee	remember that Jesus told you all this would happen	(Mary sees Jesus; mistakes him for gardener at first)
reaction	fear	fear and great joy		Mary recognizes Jesus when he says her name
response	women tell no one	women tell other disciples	women tell the apostles	Mary tells the other disciples

time the gospels were written the details had become so confused or forgotten that the actual story was hopelessly lost. Or maybe you would conclude that the differences are indications that the stories were never meant to be taken literally. In any case, the many striking disparities would reinforce your doubts about the historical reliability of the stories.

It is natural for outsiders to focus on differences and the historical problems they create. But what about insiders? Do they grow skeptical of the resurrection stories when they reflect on all the differences among them? A few might begin to have some doubts, but the vast majority of insiders are not much bothered by the disparities. Insiders seldom even notice them; if they

CHART TWO

Easter Appearance Stories

	Matt 28:9–10	Luke 24:13–33	Luke 24:34	Luke 24:36–51	John 20:19–23
to whom?	women who came to tomb	two disciples	Simon	the Eleven and others	disciples
where?	between tomb and hideout	on road to Emmaus	?	a room in Jerusalem	a room in Jerusalem
reaction	they worship him	non-recognition	?	fear; mistake him for a ghost; "they disbelieve for joy"	gladness
confirmation			?	Jesus invites them to touch him; eats fish	Jesus shows them his hands and side
message	tell them to go to Galilee	(Jesus interprets scripture)	?	(Jesus interprets scripture; commissions them to preach repentance and forgiveness in his name)	(conferral of Holy Spirit and authority to forgive and retain sins)
conclusion		they recognize him as he breaks bread; he vanishes; they return to Jerusalem	?	Jesus leads them to Bethany and ascends into heaven *(end of gospel)*	

do, they do not regard them as real inconsistencies. In fact, some apologists can even flip these differences over and use them to increase insiders' confidence in the historical reliability of the stories. They do this by arguing that, even with all the disparities, the versions all still agree that some followers of Jesus found his tomb empty.

The point I am making is that while insiders and outsiders may read the same stories, they will use very different standards in evaluating their historical reliability. Imagine that another religion had a story about how God had

CHART THREE
Post-Easter Appearance Stories

	Matt 28:16–20	John 20:26–29	John 21	Acts 1:1–11
when?	?	one week later	some time later	over a forty-day period
to whom?	the Eleven	disciples (including Thomas)	seven disciples	the Apostles
where?	a mountain in Galilee	a room in Jerusalem	the Sea of Tiberias	Jerusalem
reaction	some worship him; some doubt		recognition	
confirmation		Jesus invites Thomas to touch him		
message	the Great Commission	blessing on those who believe without seeing	to Peter: feed my lambs; discussion of fate of Beloved Disciple	wait for Holy Spirit; be my witnesses
conclusion	*(end of gospel)*		*(end of gospel)*	Jesus ascends into heaven

worked mighty miracles that demonstrated the truth of that religion. Imagine also that there were several versions of this story and that these versions had numerous discrepancies, inconsistencies, and contradictions. Wouldn't you, a Christian and thus an outsider to this religion, point to those disparities as evidence for the unreliability of these stories? People are naturally more charitably inclined to their own stories than they are to those of outsiders.

To consider a specific example, how many non-Mormons take seriously the story about Joseph Smith discovering the golden tablets that contained the Book of Mormon and deciphering them with spectacles made of stone? Non-Mormons find this story unbelievable, if not mildly amusing. But most Mormons find it easy to believe and those few with doubts can overcome them by strengthening their faith through prayer. Why should non-Mormons find the story hard to believe? After all, it is no more implausible than dozens of stories in the Bible (for example, Jonah and the whale) that many Christians believe with no difficulty at all. The difference has very little to do with the stories themselves and a great deal to do with whether one approaches them as an insider or an outsider. Putting it a bit crudely perhaps, stories about *our* miracles are easy to believe because they're true; stories about *their* miracles are easy to dismiss because they're farfetched and fictitious.

WHY DON'T APOLOGIES SUCCEED?

Why is it that very few, if any, outsiders are persuaded by apologies? They often give the impression that nobody who is informed, rational, and sincere could disagree with them. So why don't they work? Apologists seldom have a good answer to this question because there are really only two alternatives: the apology fails to convince either 1) because it is unpersuasive, or 2) because outsiders defeat the truth, usually by reasoning incorrectly and drawing the wrong conclusion, or by seeing the truth but not accepting it. In other words, there is a defect either in the apology or in the "apologee," and since few apologists present an argument they believe is defective, they are more or less forced to blame the apologee for failing to see, or to admit, the truth.

(This actually happened to me. Several years ago I was at dinner with several seminary professors. One of them, a professor of philosophy, was explaining his argument for the divinity of Jesus. He presented it as if only irrational people could disagree with it. I found it unpersuasive and asked him why he thought this was, He volunteered that I was informed and intelligent. When I pressed him as to why he thought I nevertheless was unconvinced by his apology, he replied that the reason might be that I was a sinner. The others at the table were visibly embarrassed, and an awkward silence lasted several long seconds. We moved on to another topic after I admitted being a sinner and then asked him if that made me any different from him.)

The problem with blaming the apologee is that not only is that self-serving, it is also gratuitous. What evidence is there that the apologee is not smart enough to follow the apologist's reasoning, or not sincere enough to want to know the truth, or not honest enough to admit it? The only answer the apologist can give is that if the apologee really were rational and well intentioned, he or she would agree with the apologist. Needless to say, most people are not impressed by this line of reasoning.

I used to think this way myself when I was a true believer in the power of apologetics. I was a philosophy major at a Catholic college. I was utterly convinced not only that Christianity was the one true religion that God intended for all humanity, but also that the Catholic Church was the one true church that Christ intended for all Christians. From my study of Thomas Aquinas and modern Christian apologists, I clearly saw that the central truths of Christianity (and of Catholicism) could be grasped by reason, if only one was sincerely seeking God's truth, was humble enough to accept it, and took the time to inform oneself and follow the arguments.

All of this made perfect sense to me and none of my teachers or fellow students (all of whom were Catholics) gave me any reason to question it. I tried out various apologetic arguments on my like-minded friends, who found them quite convincing. Occasionally they suggested improvements in my arguments, but none of us doubted the effectiveness of apologetics. The only real puzzle in my mind was, since the truths of Christianity and Catholicism are so evident, why are they not more universally recognized? I concluded that those outside my religion or my church just did not know or did not understand these apologetic arguments, or that they were not completely sincere about seeking the truth. It amazes me now that I believed this without any feelings of superiority or smugness. I was sincerely grateful to God for the blessing of having been raised in the Christian religion and the one true church and I prayed for the wisdom and the courage to be able to help others to see the truth as clearly as I did.

This mind-set held together until I went to graduate school at secular universities and I associated with people from different religions. For the first time in my life, I got to know people who took other religions as seriously as I took mine. I knew these people were well educated and highly rational, and I could tell from our conversations that they were sincere. A few were people of deep spirituality and great goodness. Yet none of them was persuaded by my apologetics. It took several years, but gradually I accepted the fact that informed, intelligent, sincere, and spiritual people are almost never persuaded by apologetics to change their core beliefs. Looking back, I can now see that a big reason for this is that most apologetics use assumptions that only insiders take for granted.* It is usually only from an outsider's perspective that one can see how problematic these assumptions really are.

---

* In William Craig's rebuttal of my response in *Will the Real Jesus Please Stand Up?*, he quotes my statement here and responds directly to it. "Dr. Miller says that the 'big reason' that 'informed, intelligent, sincere, and spiritual people are almost never persuaded by apologetics' is that 'most apologists use assumptions that only insiders take for granted.' I suspect that this answer is far too intellectualist, that all sorts of emotional, social, and moral factors also conspire to block the efficacy of an argument" (p. 176). Craig's response is interesting in that it precisely confirms my analysis of

In summary, apologies almost never reach outsiders. When they do, they are almost never taken seriously; when they are, they are almost never persuasive. So, if the purpose of apologetics is to convince outsiders to adopt new beliefs, then apologies are almost always abject failures. They fail, not because their authors are inept (many of them are intelligent thinkers and capable writers), but because it is practically impossible to argue people into giving up their religious beliefs and adopting new ones.

However, there is another, more promising way to evaluate the apologetic genre. We can determine its audience, not by whom it *seems* to be aimed at, but by who *actually* reads apologetic works. And we can determine an apology's purpose, not by what the author seems to intend, but by how it actually functions. If we proceed like this, we reach two important findings: 1) the audience for an apology is insiders; 2) its function is to support what the audience already believes.

This is nothing new to apologists, who know full well that their audiences are insiders. After all, the vast majority of books on Christian apologetics are published by companies that specialize in books that appeal to conservative Christians. Nor is it a coincidence that professors of apologetics teach at Christian colleges and seminaries. So why do apologists write as if they were addressing outsiders? They do that, not because they are mistaken about their audience, but because that is the convention of the apologetic genre. An apt comparison is the genre of the open letter. An open letter may begin, "To the President of the United States," but both author and readers understand that the real audience is the general public. Readers don't think they are reading the president's mail. Everyone knows the difference between an open letter and a personal letter that is leaked to the press. The public knows the open letter is intended for them, even though it is addressed to the president. Every genre has its own conventions. Authors of fables write about talking animals because that is how fables go, not because anyone thinks that animals really talk.

Acquaintance with the conventions of apologetics helps us understand what an apology for the resurrection is really about. Since it is meant for insiders, even though it seems to be addressed to outsiders, we have to distinguish its message (that is, its message to its real audience) from its content. Its content is an argument aimed at convincing outsiders that they should believe in the resurrection literally because that is the rational thing to do; indeed, to do otherwise would be irrational. But the message to the

how an apologist explains the failure of his apology: if you are not persuaded by the argument, there must be something wrong with *you*.

real audience is that their belief in Jesus is far more than wishful thinking; it is founded on solid evidence and can be defended by someone with impressive academic credentials. Critical scholars can point out historical problems in the gospels, but apologists have answers for all of them. Apologetics reassures insiders that they can be confident in the literal truth of their belief in the resurrection, despite any doubts raised by those who question it.

It should now be clear that *in order to understand what a text is really about, we need to take into account who its audience is and how it functions for that audience.* Only after we figure out these elements can we make an informed judgment about what the message of the text is.

Let's apply this to the resurrection stories in the gospels.* Who is the audience for these stories? What did their authors think they were doing in writing the way they did? And how did these stories function for their audience?

THE AUDIENCE OF THE GOSPELS

Apologists treat these gospel stories as literal accounts of what really happened. These are stories about how faith in the resurrection got started: the earliest Christians believed that Jesus was raised because some of them had actually seen him in his physical body after his death. Apologists argue that if people today properly understand these stories, they will conclude that Jesus was physically raised from the dead, and from this they will conclude that Jesus is God. Apologists fold these gospel stories into their own arguments, which seem aimed at outsiders but are actually for believers. Apologies thus appear to be intended to induce faith, but actually function to confirm the faith of those who already believe.

We need to ask: Who was the original audience of the gospels? For whom did the evangelists write? The answer is clear: the gospels were written for Christians. They presuppose that their audiences already believe in Jesus. Although a few outsiders may have read a gospel, it is most unlikely that any of them came to believe in Jesus by reading these texts. This is especially so in the case of the resurrection stories. How likely is it that a Jew or a pagan would have read one of these stories and then concluded that Jesus had been physically raised from the dead and that therefore he was God? No, the res-

---

* Strictly speaking, there are no resurrection narratives in the New Testament. That is, there are no stories that tell of Jesus coming back to life and emerging from the tomb. All four gospels have stories about his followers finding his tomb empty and three gospels have stories about Jesus appearing to his followers after his death. (The gospel that Mark wrote ended at 16:8 with the women fleeing the tomb; the stories in Mark 16:9–20 were added in the second century.)

urrection stories presume a friendly audience, people who already believed that Jesus had risen. The stories build on and presuppose that belief in order to teach about the meaning of Jesus' resurrection and its implications for Christian life.

To get specific about what the evangelists are trying to communicate in the resurrection stories, we need to focus on one specific gospel as an example. Any one will do, but Matthew is especially appropriate because some features unique to this gospel give us strong clues about its author's intentions.

THE RESURRECTION OF THE RIGHTEOUS JEWS

A fascinating peculiarity of Matthew's gospel is that it tells of other resurrections in addition to Jesus'. According to Matthew, many righteous Jews were raised from the dead along with Jesus. At the very moment that Jesus died,

> the earth quaked, rocks were split apart, and the tombs were opened, and many bodies of sleeping saints came back to life. And they came out of the tombs after his resurrection and went into the holy city, where they appeared to many. (Matt 27:51–53)

What should we make of this strange story? Did it really happen? And what does it mean?

We need to take a close look at this brief account because it can tell us a great deal about what Matthew thought he was writing and what his audience thought they were reading. The first question we have to tackle is whether this story is historical.

To put it bluntly, there is no good reason to think that this event really happened. It is mentioned nowhere else—not in another gospel, not in any other Christian writing, not in the writings of Josephus (a well-informed and meticulous Jewish historian of the time). In most cases it is invalid to conclude that an event did not happen simply because it is mentioned in only one source—after all, lots of things occur that are not recorded even once. But this story is a very special exception to the rule because it narrates what by any measure has to be the most amazing event of all time: large numbers of dead people coming to life and appearing to large numbers of witnesses. It is inconceivable that an event so sensational and of such magnitude would not be noticed by the historians of the day. It's especially inconceivable that no other Christian source would mention it. The people who had left their tombs on Easter would have been hugely famous among Christians. A few lucky disciples could claim to have seen the risen Jesus, but these people were even more privileged: they had been raised from the dead *along with* Jesus. Yet their story left no trace anywhere outside these three short verses in Matthew.

It is virtually impossible to explain why Paul does not mention this event if it had actually happened. In 1 Cor 15:5–8, Paul emphasizes the reality of Jesus' resurrection by listing those who had experienced the risen Jesus. How could he fail to mention those who had experienced their own resurrections as a result of his? Furthermore, Paul refers to the risen Jesus as "the first fruits of those who have fallen asleep" (1 Cor 15:20). The imagery of first fruits implies that Jesus was the only one raised. (Paul writes that Jesus *is* the first fruits, not that he is *among* the first fruits.) Paul also teaches that the just will be raised only when Jesus returns to earth. If Paul knew of the event Matthew relates, the logic of his first fruits metaphor would be ruined. Paul's train of thought shows that he did not know about the event Matthew narrates.

Unless one is committed to belief in the literal historicity of every passage in the Bible, there is no basis for taking Matt 27:51–53 to be the report of an actual event. Does this mean that Matthew was misinformed, or that he was lying? Not at all. Matthew never intended this account to be taken literally. He assumed that his audience would take it symbolically and understand its message accordingly.

What is that message? Two features of this brief narrative furnish clues that would have been clear to Matthew's readers: the earthquake and the way Matthew characterizes those who come back to life. Both features signalled to Matthew's readers that the death and resurrection of Jesus is *the* decisive event in salvation history, the event that ushers in the time of the fulfillment of God's plans for humanity. This scene has the same message as twelve other scenes in which Matthew interrupts the gospel narrative to tell the readers that a certain event fulfills what was foretold by the prophets: that God's promises to Israel are coming true in Jesus, that Jesus (in his birth, life, death, and resurrection) is the culmination of Israel's hopes and of God's plans for His people.

One feature in Matt 27:51–53 that conveys Matthew's message is how he describes those who are raised from the dead: he calls them "holy ones" or "saints" (*hagioi* in Greek). This designation is important because early Christians and most Jews believed that those who had lived in obedience to

God's will would be raised from the dead on the Last Day. Matt 27:51–53 thus sends the message that Jesus' death and resurrection was the beginning of the End, the apocalyptic turning point in salvation history.*

The earthquake is the other feature that conveys Matthew's message in Matt 27:51–53. Earthquakes are one of the disasters that prophetic and apocalyptic writings associate with the arrival of the End. These cataclysmic events are used to symbolize the enormous importance and consequences of God's intervention in our history. (We still use this imagery in much the same way today when we speak of an "earth shaking" event. Everyone knows we are not referring to a literal earthquake.) Matthew's mention of an earthquake in 27:51 also helps him explain how the tombs were opened. He uses this symbol again at the scene on Easter morning (28:2), even though he does not need it to explain how Jesus' tomb was opened. As Matthew tells it, an angel rolled away the stone, but Matthew adds the earthquake nonetheless, thereby linking Jesus' resurrection with those in 27:51–53. Jesus' tomb was already empty, so the earthquake is doubly unnecessary here. Its sole function in 28:2 is as an apocalyptic symbol.

Biblical authors intentionally used disasters like earthquakes as symbols. This can be seen clearly in Acts 2, where Luke tells the story of the first Pentecost. People are amazed that they each hear the apostles preaching in their own language (Acts 2:5–12). Peter explains that what is happening is fulfilling the prophecy of Joel. Peter then quotes a long passage from Joel, part of which reads:

> I will show portents in the heavens above and signs on the earth below: blood, and fire, and vapor of smoke. The sun shall be turned to darkness and the moon to blood, before the coming of the great and glorious day of the Lord (Acts 2:19–20, quoting Joel 2:30–31).

Note that Peter claims that Joel's prophecy is being fulfilled in the events of Pentecost, not that it will be fulfilled at some future date. Obviously, Peter was not asserting that actual smoke was literally darkening the sun or turning the moon red as he spoke. Peter assumed his audience would understand these apocalyptic descriptions symbolically, and Luke expects his readers to do so as well.

---

* Knowing that this is Matthew's meaning helps us make sense of an exceedingly strange feature of the story: though the dead come to life when their tombs are opened at the death of Jesus, they do not leave their tombs until after Jesus leaves his. This makes no sense at all if it is meant to be a report of an actual event. But if the story is symbolic, it is only fitting that Jesus be the first to leave the abode of the dead—even if Matthew partially compromises Jesus' priority by having others come back to life before him.

Historians have no real choice but to conclude that the resurrections mentioned in Matt 27:51–53 did not really happen. There is just no objective evidence for the historicity of the event. Except for those already committed to literalism, very, very few biblical scholars would argue that Matt 27:51–53 is historical. (It would be interesting to poll evangelical scholars for their position on this and their reasons for it.)

To sum up, we can reach the same conclusion on the historicity of Matt 27:51–53 from two directions. On the one hand, we have no objective basis for claiming that the event really happened. On the other hand, we have strong clues from the way Matthew writes the story that he never intended it to be taken literally.

WHAT DID MATTHEW THINK HE WAS WRITING?

If Matthew can create historical fiction like the resurrection of the righteous Jews, what does that mean for the other stories in his gospel? Obviously, this by itself does not require skepticism about every scene in the gospels. Because one story is fictitious it does not mean that all of them are. Perhaps, then, Matt 27:51–53 is an anomaly,* a passage where Matthew proceeds in a way totally unlike the way he writes in the rest of his gospel. If so, it can tell us nothing about the evangelists' overall perspective on the kind of truth they intended to communicate. But there is no good reason to regard Matt 27:51–53 as an anomaly. Matthew weaves this scene seamlessly into his narration of the death of Jesus. The clues in the scene that Matthew did not intend the story to be understood literally do not signal that this is the *only* such scene in his gospel. Thus the fictitious nature of 27:51–53 is neither grounds for the one extreme position of skepticism about everything in the gospel nor for the opposite extreme of considering it a unique aberration. There is simply no reason to reverse our natural assumption that if an author writes fiction in one scene, he may well have written it in others.

Since historical fiction is part of Matthew's literary repertoire, it means that we have to read his gospel (and all the gospels) with the knowledge that

---

* This is the position Craig takes in his rebuttal to my response in *Will the Real Jesus Please Stand Up?* He argues that while the apocalyptic coloring of this scene indicates that it is not to be taken literally, the empty tomb story is "remarkable just for its its simplicity and lack of apocalyptic embellishment" (p. 165). But all the elements of 27:51–53 (an earthquake opening tombs, dead bodies coming back to life, and resurrected people leaving their tombs and appearing to witnesses) also figure in the Easter story. Matthew does not explicitly narrate Jesus' body coming back to life or him leaving the tomb, but he obviously presupposes it: that's why the tomb is empty. How can the same apocalyptic elements indicate fiction in one scene and fact in another?

the gospel genre includes both historical fact and historical fiction. If we take this seriously, we cannot presume that the evangelists regarded historical accuracy as their primary objective. Knowing that Matthew invented fictional stories is a crucial clue that can help us understand Matthew's (and the other evangelists') perspective toward the historical value of the stories in the gospel.

To gauge how Matthew regarded the historicity of the events he narrates, we have to keep in mind that Matthew relies on Mark as one of his sources. Sometimes he virtually copies from Mark, sometimes he paraphrases. Sometimes he abbreviates Mark's narrative, deleting non-essential details while retaining the substance of the story. At other times though, Matthew deliberately alters Mark. He does not simply reword the account, but he changes its content in such a way as to alter Mark's meaning, sometimes a little, sometimes a lot; sometimes subtly, sometimes obviously.

An unusually clear example is the way in which Matt 20:20–23 alters Mark 10:35–40. Mark tells of Jesus teaching his disciples that he will be put to death in Jerusalem (Mark 10:33–34). James and John then approach Jesus with the request that he grant them the places of highest honor when he comes into his glory. Because they had just heard Jesus' prediction of his passion, their request appears incredibly crass and shows that James and John totally failed to grasp the meaning of Jesus' teaching. When Matthew tells this story, he has the mother of James and John make the brazen request on behalf of her sons (Matt 20:20). Why did Matthew make this change? Did he think that Mark was historically wrong at this point and that his own version gives the real story of what had actually happened? There is not the slightest indication that Matthew made this change to set the record straight. Mark has a number of other scenes in which the disciples act stupidly or selfishly and each time Matthew alters these scenes in such a way that the disciples act wisely and behave as role models for Christians (see, for example, the disciples' response to Jesus in Mark 6:51–52 and in Matt 14:32–33). In Matt 20:20–23 Matthew's small but significant modification enables him to retain the valuable lesson the scene teaches, but without besmirching the reputation of these two famous apostles.

There are dozens and dozens of places where Matthew alters Mark. Careful analysis of these changes (a process called redaction criticism) helps us to understand the messages Matthew is communicating through his distinctive version of the words and deeds of Jesus. These changes show beyond the shadow of a doubt that Matthew felt free to change Mark's story when he did not agree with some aspect of its message or when he believed his changes would make it a better vehicle for his own message. These changes show either that Matthew did not regard Mark's gospel as a literal report of actual events, or that he did not care one way or the other. For Matthew (and by extrapolation, for all the evangelists) facts were far less important than the meanings they expressed—after all, the facts could be changed to enhance the message.

Turning to the Easter stories, we can see how Matthew has altered Mark's version of the scene at the empty tomb. Two women (not three, as in Mark) go to see the tomb (not to anoint the body) before sunrise (not after). As they arrive there is an earthquake, during which an angel rolls away the stone, terrifying the guards. (In Mark the women find the stone already rolled away when they arrive; Mark mentions neither an earthquake, nor an angel, nor guards.) Matthew's angel speaks to the women from outside the tomb; in Mark a young man speaks to them after they step inside. The scene in Matthew concludes when the women, instead of fleeing in fear and telling no one (as in Mark), "depart in fear and great joy" and tell the disciples.

Matthew does not think Mark was misinformed. He is not trying to set the record straight. It is not a question of whether Matthew is right and Mark is wrong or vice versa. Matthew does not think that Mark gave a literal report of an actual event, and there's no good reason for us to think that Matthew considered his own version to be a literal report either.

Matthew did not write his account to prove that Jesus' resurrection is a fact of history. Did Matthew believe that there was a historical kernel to his story that was literally true? That is, did he believe that Jesus had in fact been buried, that people knew where, and that some women had discovered the tomb to be empty? Maybe he did; maybe he didn't. We really don't know and *there is no way of telling from the gospel he wrote* some fifty years after Jesus' death. All we do know is that Matthew inherited this story from Mark and felt free to alter it considerably in order to proclaim his faith in Jesus' resurrection. And that, it seems to me, is the key: faith. The evangelists are interested in faith far more than in facts. We also know that they felt free to invent facts by creating stories out of whole cloth if this would enhance their proclamation of faith.

CAN FICTION EXPRESS TRUTH?

Our consideration of the story about the earthquake and the rising of the Jewish saints in Matt 27:51–53 leads to the conclusion that it is not the report of an actual event, that Matthew did not intend it to be, and that his ancient audience understood that.

So is the story false? That depends on the precise meaning of the question. If it means, "Is the story a fiction, a narrative of an event that did not in fact happen?," the answer is "Yes, it is false." But if the question means, "Is what the author intends to communicate false?," then we have to ask a more basic question: Is Matthew's message false simply because the story he used to convey it is not historical? Matthew's meaning is that the death and resurrection of Jesus is *the* turning point in salvation history, God's decisive intervention in human affairs. Are we being inconsistent if we profess the truth of Matthew's message *and* acknowledge that Matt 27:51–53 is not historical?

Well, millions of Christians believe Matthew's message without actually knowing the story in Matt 27:51–53. (In my long experience as a Bible teacher, I have found that many Christians are surprised when they encounter this story. Even many of those familiar with the Bible say things like, "I don't remember reading this before.") This was all the more so in the first century, when very few Christians had access to Matthew's gospel. Mark, Luke, John, Paul, and the other New Testament authors surely agreed with Matthew that Jesus' death and resurrection were God's decisive act in salvation history, even though nothing indicates that they knew the story related in Matt 27:51–53.

Another way of getting at the issue is to ask which came first, the story or the belief in its message? Does Matthew's story provide the basis for the belief that Jesus' death and resurrection are the decisive event in salvation history, or does the story express this belief? In other words, which caused which? Did the story give rise to the belief or did the belief give rise to the story? In light of our historical considerations, the answer is clear: the story presumes and expresses the belief in its message. Matthew (or someone in his tradition) created the story to express faith in the supreme spiritual importance of Jesus' death and resurrection. The story is addressed to an audience that believes in Jesus and so understands and believes its message.

Considering the matter from another direction also shows that the story presupposed, rather than gave rise to, faith in Jesus. At the time Matthew wrote his gospel Jesus was a very controversial figure. Virtually all Jews rejected the claim that he was the Messiah, a very few accepted it (i.e., the Christian Jews, or Jewish Christians—either term will do), but nobody was neutral about Jesus. How could one be? There was no middle ground. It is inconceivable that a serious Jew could have said, "Maybe Jesus is the Messiah, maybe he isn't; either way is all right with me." Because of the polarized religious situation, Jews who were not followers of Jesus were hostile to what they thought he stood for and to his disciples. Now, what are the realistic chances that someone like this would read or hear the story in Matt

27:51–53 and as a result conclude that Jesus must have been the one through whom God had decisively intervened in human history? The odds of that happening are even lower than the odds that any of my readers will be converted to Islam by the Muslim apologetic that I so clumsily outlined above.* Matthew's story would simply not persuade outsiders. They would understand its message, but they would immediately reject it because they would have no prior belief in Jesus. Matthew knew full well that his stories would not persuade Jews hostile to Jesus. In fact, Matt 28:11–15 tries to explain (to insiders, of course) why even those who knew Jesus' tomb was empty did not believe in his resurrection.

WHAT DOES AN EMPTY TOMB PROVE?

Try to see the situation from a Jewish perspective. Matt 28:11–15 reflects Matthew's bitter animosity toward the Jewish leaders, to whom he here imputes corrupt and deceitful motives. But if we step back from Matthew's extremely one-sided perspective, we realize that the only thing that most Jews knew about the situation was that followers of Jesus *claimed* that he had risen from the dead.

To get some idea of how this must have sounded to Jews of the time, imagine how we would respond to reports by some members of a cult that their recently deceased leader (whom they had buried) had risen. Their reports that his grave was empty would hardly persuade many. Even if it was confirmed that the grave where they claim he was buried was empty, what would that prove? Nothing. We would conclude either that they had removed the body or that he was never buried there in the first place. Suppose they told stories of seeing angels at the empty grave or of the grave being opened by an earthquake. Suppose they claimed that our leaders were involved in a conspiracy to cover up the truth about the resurrection of their master. Suppose they told of having seen him alive, of having spoken and eaten with him. And (though I can't imagine how this would come about in our society) suppose that some of these witnesses were willing to die for their belief in their leader.

What would we make of such people and their belief in their "messiah"? Probably something similar to what ancient people made of the earliest Christians. (As a thought experiment, ask yourself what it would take to convince you that this cult leader had truly risen from the dead.)

---

* I say "even lower than" rather than "the same as" because the apology at least gives a rational argument, whereas Matt 27:51–53 merely makes an unsupported assertion.

Empty tombs don't prove anything, except to insiders. Nor do reports of appearances of risen leaders. In the gospels the risen Jesus appears only to those who already believe in him. Those who see him after his resurrection are those who followed him during his lifetime. John's gospel originally ended with a blessing for those who believe in Jesus without needing to see him firsthand.* John's implication is that it takes little faith to believe when one has seen the risen Lord in person. Matthew, however, does not agree. At the very end of Matthew's gospel is a fascinating and unexpected statement. He reports that even some of the apostles who personally encountered the risen Jesus had their doubts. Just before Jesus sent forth the Eleven with the Great Commission, they prostrated themselves before Jesus, "but some doubted" (28:17). This gospel thus closes with a cryptic admission that even some of these ultimate insiders were not convinced by a face-to-face encounter with the risen Lord. Matthew's abrupt comment comes as a complete surprise and its precise meaning is puzzling. But this much at least is clear: Whatever else the gospels may teach about the resurrection, faith in the risen Jesus requires more than stories about him, no matter how convincing these stories may be to some insiders.

* See John 20:29. The original version of John's gospel ended at 20:31. Chapter 21 was added in the final edition.

NOTES

Introduction

1. "The Inside Is (Not) the Outside: Q 11:39–41 and Thomas 89." *Forum* 5 (1989), pp. 92–105; "Historical Method and the Deeds of Jesus: The Test Case of the Temple Demonstration." *Forum* 8 (1992): pp. 5–30; "Drawing a Blank from the Well: Thomas 74." *Forum* 10 (1994), pp. 95–107; "Historicizing the Trans-historical: The Transfiguration Narrative." *Forum* 10 (1994), pp. 219–48.

Chapter 1

1. The values are red: 3, pink: 2, gray: 1, black: 0. The sum of the numerical value of all the votes is divided by the number of votes cast. The result is the weighted average, which is expressed as a percentage and then matched to a color according to a scale marked off into four equal regions: black 0–.25; gray .251–.500, pink .501–.750, red .751–1.0. For example, consider a vote with the following results: 10 red, 15 pink, 10 gray, and 5 black. In this case the number of votes cast is 40 and the sum of their numerical value is 70 (30 for the ten red votes + 30 for the fifteen pink votes + 10 for the ten gray votes + 0 for the black votes). Thus, the weighted average is 1.75 (70 ÷ 40), or .58 (1.75 ÷ 3.00), which is pink.

2. "Saying" is a generic term for the utterances of Jesus. It includes parables, proverbs, aphorisms, riddles, and other speech forms. To be a "saying" an utterance must be capable of making sense on its own, apart from its literary context in the gospels. That is, it must be able to be transmitted orally as a self-contained unit of speech. Sayings do not include utterances that are not detachable from their narrative contexts. For example, "What do you want me to do for you?" (as in Mark 9:36 or 9:51) or "Your trust has cured you" (as in Mark 5:34) are, by definition, not sayings. The Seminar dealt with these kind of utterances when it considered the deeds of Jesus.

In the gospels sayings are often arranged into larger discourses (for example, the Sermon on the Mount). Since the Seminar considered each saying separately, many discourses contain sayings of different colors.

3. The difference between SV's "indignant" and NRSV's "moved with pity" is not a difference in translation. Instead, it reflects different decisions over which Greek word was in the original text of Mark 1:41. Some ancient manuscripts have the word for pity and some have the word for indignation. SV opts for "indignant" because this is the more difficult reading (*lectio difficilior*), which means that it is more likely that the difficult "indignant" would be changed by a later copyist to the easier "moved with pity" than vice-versa.

4. The most comprehensive of these studies is *The Gospel of Thomas and Jesus*, by Seminar member Stephen Patterson (Polebridge Press, 1993).

5. The best of these technical papers are revised and published as articles in the journal *Forum*.

6. For example, the authors of *The Five Gospels* are listed as "Robert W. Funk, Roy W. Hoover, and the Jesus Seminar." Funk and Hoover prepared the introductory material and wrote the commentary for this volume. Like dozens of other Fellows, Funk and Hoover also made individual scholarly contributions to the Seminar's work, but do not claim individual credit for it in *The Five Gospels*.

7. See John Hick, *The Metaphor of God Incarnate* (Westminster John Knox, 1993), pp. 27–46, for a brilliant exploration of the implications of this development..

8. In Matt 8:17, the evangelist quotes Isa 53:4 and applies it to Jesus, but in reference to his healings, not to his suffering and death. Furthermore, Matthew does not claim that it was Jesus who quoted this verse or connected it to his ministry. The only other explicit application in the New

Testament of a Suffering Servant passage to Jesus is attributed to the apostle Philip in Acts 8:35.

9. See C. K. Barrett, "The Background of Mark 10:45," in *New Testament Essays: Studies in Memory of Thomas Walter Manson* (Manchester: Manchester University Press, 1959), pp. 1–18. Also, Morna Hooker, *Jesus and the Servant: The Influence of the Servant Concept of Deutero-Isaiah in the New Testament* (London: SPCK, 1959), pp. 74–83.

Chapter 2

1. The relevant passage in the Qur'an is 4:157.

2. See *The Five Gospels*, pp. 289–90.

3. See *The Five Gospels*, p. 355.

4. For a lucid exposition of the assumptions and methods commonly used in critical research of the historical Jesus, see Stephen J. Patterson, *The God of Jesus* (Trinity Press International, 1998), pp. 251–74.

Chapter 3

1. *The Five Gospels* contains the Gospels of Mark, Matthew, Luke, and John, plus the Gospel of Thomas. *The Acts of Jesus* includes the four canonical gospels, a few passages from Acts of the Apostles and 1 Corinthians that report resurrection appearances, plus the full text of the Gospel of Peter, which tells of Jesus' trial, death, and resurrection.

2. There is another official definition of these meanings in *The Five Gospels*.

> Red   I would include this item unequivocally in the database for deter
> mining who Jesus was.
>
> Pink   I would include this item with reservations (or modifications) in
> the database.
>
> Gray   I would not include this item in the database, but I might make use
> of some of the content in determining who Jesus was.
>
> Black   I would not include this item in the primary database.

Obviously, these two sets of definitions are roughly equivalent. I use the other definitions in my discussion because it is my impression that Seminar members preferred them and seldom relied on the formulations printed in this note.

3. In four cases (Mark 10:6–8, 10:19, 11:17, 12:29–31) enough Fellows had reasons to attribute these quotations to Jesus himself to produce a gray result.

4. The voting results for the sayings are tabulated in exacting detail in the Voting Records in volumes 6 and 7 of *Forum*.

5. Not counting parallel versions, these are Mark 1:23–28, 5:1–20, 7:24–30, 9:14–29; Matt 9:32–34, 12:22–23.

Chapter 4

1. "The Corrected Jesus." *First Things* (May 1994), pp. 43–48.

2. "The Jesus Seminar's misguided quest for the historical Jesus." *Christian Century* (January 3–10, 1996), pp. 16–22.

3. "A Century of Quests for the Culturally Compatible Jesus." *Theology Today* 25 (April 1995), pp. 17–28.

4. "The Gospel According to the Jesus Seminar." *Religion* 25 (1995), pp. 317–38.

5. "Jesus, the Talking Head." Chapter 2 in *The Jesus Quest* (Downers Grove, Ill.: InterVarsity Press, 1995).

6. *The Jesus Quest*, p. 44.

7. Voting among biblical scholars to determine consensus on issues of translation and textual criticism is uncontroversial, even if it is a relatively recent practice. But the tradition of voting among ecclesial authorities to determine official doctrines about the Bible is much more ancient. For example, the Catholic Church formally adopted the contents of Jerome's Vulgate as the canon of the

Bible at the Council of Trent. The vote among the bishops in attendance was 23 for, 15 against, with 16 abstentions.

Voting does carry a potential for misrepresentation if all that is published is the final result, for this might give the appearance of unanimity when in fact some votes may have been close calls. This is why the United Bible Society uses its A-B-C-D rating system and why the Jesus Seminar publishes the percentage of red, pink, gray, and black votes for each individual item.

8. "The Jesus Seminar's misguided quest," p. 17.

9. "The Corrected Jesus," p. 47.

10. "A Century of Quests," p. 27.

11. I did find three items in *The Five Gospels* that should be mentioned in this context. First, there is this assertion on p. 35: "the kind of scholarship represented by the Fellows of the Jesus Seminar is the kind that has come to prevail in all the great universities of the world." In its context, this clearly means that the kind of scholarship practiced by the Seminar is *critical* scholarship, as opposed to dogmatic or apologetic scholarship. This statement cannot be taken for a claim that the specific methods or results of the Seminar would be endorsed by a majority of critical scholars. Second, Robert Funk's discussion of the "fifth pillar" of "scholarly wisdom" (pp. 3–4) can rightly be taken as an implicit claim that most scholars no longer view Jesus as an eschatological figure. Such a claim is questionable. Third, the mention of an early version of the Gospel of Thomas presents a controversial thesis as a bland fact. However, none of these three entries amounts to the kind of claim that Hays and Kee allege.

In a letter responding to my inquiry, Richard Hays identified two sentences in *The Five Gospels* (one of them is the one from p. 35 that I quote above) that, if taken out of context, might mislead uncritical readers. He also wrote to me that the Seminar has claimed repeatedly to represent the scholarly consensus in its public statements, as documented in Luke Johnson's book, *The Real Jesus*. In his book Johnson excerpts dozens of statements culled from newspaper clippings. These are all brief remarks, many not even full sentences, all quoted out of context. To be sure, Seminar members have said some dumb things to the press. And Robert Funk, who frequently acts as spokesman for the Seminar and who is quoted more than all other members put together, tends to speak provocatively. Even so, I could not find more than one or two statements that even *seem* to make this claim. (The closest one comes to it is in headlines, such as "Jesus did not predict his own second coming, scholars say." But as we all know, headlines are written by journalists, not scholars.)

12. Ben Witherington attacks the Seminar for being "a *very carefully* self-selected group" (*The Jesus Quest*, p. 43, emphasis added). A group that accepts all qualified applicants cannot control who joins. "Very carefully self-selected" is a self-contradiction.

13. "The Jesus Seminar's misguided quest," p. 16.

14. "The Corrected Jesus," p. 47. Hays' list was accurate when it was published. Since then, Karen King, a seminar member since its founding, has joined the faculty of Harvard Divinity School.

15. "The Jesus Seminar's misguided quest," p. 16. Johnson errs in adding Emory to the list of institutions without faculty representation in the Jesus Seminar. Vernon Robbins, a well-known New Testament scholar and a colleague of Johnson's at Emory, made important contributions to the work of the Seminar and is listed as a Fellow of the Seminar in *The Five Gospels*.

16. "The Corrected Jesus," p. 47.

17. "A Century of Quests," p. 25 (emphasis added).

18. "The Gospel According to the Jesus Seminar," p. 322 (emphasis added).

19. Only Luke Johnson rejects this premise. But he rejects the legitimacy of all historical Jesus research (see the next chapter). Commenting on the presence of Thomas in *The Five Gospels*, he charges, "Its inclusion seems to make primarily a political or 'culture wars' point: the Gospels are to be considered of value only insofar as they are sources for the historical Jesus" ("The Jesus Seminar's misguided quest," pp. 19–20). Johnson didn't need to guess why the Seminar included Thomas; he could have asked.

20. "The Gospel According to the Jesus Seminar," p. 322.

21. "A Century of Quests," p. 25.

22. "The Corrected Jesus," pp. 45 and 47.

23. "The Jesus Seminar's misguided quest," p. 22.

24. At this point, it is tempting to follow a tangent on the topic of how we can know what "really happened" in the Jesus Seminar. There are numerous eyewitnesses to the Seminar's events, first-person reports from participants like me, the work of various contributors to *The Five Gospels* and *The Acts of Jesus*, and Robert Funk, the redactor-author of these two books. In short, many aspects of the writing of *The Five Gospels* and *The Acts of Jesus* are tantalizingly similar to the process we presuppose for the writing of the ancient gospels. It would not even be inappropriate to characterize Bob Funk as a kind of evangelist for the historical Jesus. So while the Seminar tried to figure out what "really happened" in the life of Jesus, a vaguely analogous problem can arise when we try to figure out what "really happened" in the Jesus Seminar. But, to pursue this question further would divert us from our present topic.

25. *The Jesus Quest*, p. 55 (emphasis added).

26. "The Gospel According to the Jesus Seminar," p. 324.

27. "The Gospel According to the Jesus Seminar," p. 330.

28. "The Gospel According to the Jesus Seminar," p. 333.

29. "The Gospel According to the Jesus Seminar," p. 330.

30. "The Gospel According to the Jesus Seminar," p. 332.

31. "The Corrected Jesus," p. 47.

32. "The Gospel According to the Jesus Seminar," p. 334.

33. Witherington has a more qualified, but less intelligible, characterization of the Seminar's Jesus: "a Jesus who is a sage, but not a *very* Jewish one" (*The Jesus Quest*, p. 50, emphasis added), "who does not fit very well into the context of early Judaism" (p. 43). Calling the Seminar's Jesus "not very Jewish" means that Witherington must see him as somewhat Jewish, but since Witherington does not explain himself on this point, his criticism is as empty as the "not Jewish" one.

34. Some critics who make this accusation seem to insinuate that the Seminar is anti-Semitic. Jewish members of the Seminar may be in a better position to address this, but from my perspective this insinuation would simply be preposterous if it were not so ugly.

35. A few gray items even received a majority of red and pink votes. These statistical anomalies are the result of the Seminar's system for averaging votes, which weighs everyone's vote, not only the votes of those in the majority (see pp. 12–13 above and p. 37 of *The Five Gospels*). N.T. Wright has drawn attention to this "flaw" in our procedure to support his verdict that "A voting system like this . . . has nothing whatever to commend it" (*Jesus and the Victory of God*, Fortress, 1996, p. 34). Our system for averaging votes is not perfect, but it is better than any other system we know. In fact, the "problem" Wright points to is quite small: out of the 518 sayings the Seminar analyzed, 15 sayings (less than 3% of the total) with slight majorities of red and pink votes are colored gray.

For a full discussion of the problems with our voting process, see pp. 47–57.

Chapter 5

1. N. T. Wright's endorsement of the book on its dust jacket is especially enthusiastic: "every sentence" in the book possesses "scholarly rigor;" the book has "intellectual power" and "scholarly precision." However, in an interview with *Time* magazine shortly after the book was published, Wright concluded that Johnson's approach is fundamentally mistaken. Johnson "kicks the ball back into his own net by mistake. He's putting the clocks back to the 1890s, when the Germans said that all this historical Jesus nonsense shows we shouldn't be trying to find the Jesus behind the Gospels at all" (*Time* [April 8, 1996], p. 58).

2. Johnson actually claims they are *not* outsiders. "One would think that such a critical agenda . . . would come from outsiders . . . But such is not the case. The only real outsider among these authors is Stephen Mitchell" (p. 55). Readers must judge whether Johnson's weak disclaimer is contradicted by his assessment of the loyalties of these authors.

3. The resurrection is the necessary and sufficient cause of the religious movement, *as well as* the literature that it generated" (p. 136, emphasis added). Burton Mack astutely describes this circular-

ity (which he calls a "Catch 22") and analyzes its theological importance in *Who Wrote the New Testament?* (HarperSanFrancisco, 1995), pp. 5–16.

4. Johnson's lament over "the academic captivity of the Church" (p. 169) makes me wonder which churchgoers he talks to. I speak frequently in adult education programs in churches and I seldom encounter Christians who have more than a dim awareness of the historical-critical approach to the Bible (and this among the tiny minority of church members who participate in adult education). Ironically, the only religious education group I have met who had a solid grasp of the historical-critical study of the gospels was Jewish.

5. The Jesus Seminar would do well to take this more seriously. Indeed, I criticized my fellow Seminar members on just this point in a keynote address at one of our 1996 meetings. I believe the Seminar needs to communicate more emphatically that *all* historical results are reconstructions (see pp. 41–42). The attention-grabbing questions on the covers of our two major books ("What Did Jesus Really Say?" and "What Did Jesus Really Do?") may be elements of good marketing, but I fret that they might reinforce uncritical assumptions in our readers.

Chapter 6

1. This last point is not stated explicitly, but is the clear upshot of his argument on pp. 154–57.

2. The textual variants in Mark 1:41 are a curious anomaly: is Jesus' reaction to the leper one of pity or anger? The United Bible Society third critical edition of the Greek New Testament prints that Jesus looked at the man with "pity" (*splagchnistheis*), but gives this word a "D" rating, its lowest level of certainty. A few ancient manuscripts read that Jesus looked at the man with "anger" (*orgistheis*). This reading is far more difficult to understand and so is probably more original.

3. This theme is played out in John (see John 11:45–53), but not in Mark.

4. Again, whether Johnson makes this move intentionally is irrelevant.

5.· See pp. 54–55, for example.

6. For an elegant analysis of how Matthew combines several soteriological perspectives that resist harmonization, see David Seeley, *Deconstructing the New Testament* (Biblical Interpretation 5; Leiden: Brill, 1994), pp. 21–52, esp. pp. 48–52.

7. See Robert J. Miller, "Prophecy and Persecution in Luke-Acts" (Ph.D. diss., Claremont Graduate School, 1985), pp. 268–72.

8. Note, for example, the careful distinction in Luke 24:20: "our chief priests and leaders handed him over to be condemned to death and crucified him." In the speeches in Acts, however, Christian spokesmen repeatedly identify all the people of Israel as the killers of Jesus (e.g., Acts 1:22–23, 1:36, 3:14–15, 4:27, 7:51–52, 10:39).

9. For a lucid explication of Luke's presentation of Jesus' death as a national tragedy interpreted against the background of Jewish prophecy, see David L. Tiede, *Prophecy and History in Luke-Acts* (Philadelphia: Fortress, 1980), pp. 65–96.

10. See Miller, "Prophecy and Persecution," pp. 257–86.

11. I presume that Johnson expresses himself somewhat loosely here, since he argues earlier in the book (pp. 112–17) for the historicity of some very basic facts, such as the existence of Jesus and his crucifixion. More precisely, then, Johnson maintains that Christian faith depends on the establishment of *some* facts about the past, but only on those that Johnson believes are beyond dispute.

12. This is not the place to argue this well-known position in the philosophy of religion. Those who are interested in a full and profound treatment of this understanding of religious experience can study *An Interpretation of Religion* by John Hick (New Haven: Yale University, 1989).

13. Johnson acknowledges that some traditional material used by the evangelists contains other patterns, but holds that these patterns are not endowed with the authoritative status of the one dominant pattern. "These elements of the Jesus tradition are not made normative in the way that the pattern of obedient suffering and loving service is" (p. 166).

14. He refers to the establishment of the four-gospel canon as the Church's "affirmation of the fourfold Gospels in all their factual diversity and disagreement" (p. 148).

15. "This pattern was not a late invention but rather *an early memory*, perhaps the earliest of for-

mative memories, concerning 'the real Jesus'" (p. 162, emphasis added). The reference to "memories concerning 'the real Jesus'" is confusing inasmuch as Johnson's "real Jesus" is a figure of the present, not the past.

Chapter 7

1. Witherington makes this criticism, not in *The Jesus Quest*, but in a debate between him and me in *Bible Review*. See "Battling Over the Jesus Seminar: Buyer Beware." *Bible Review* 13.2 (April 1997), p. 24.

2. Witherington distorts the Seminar's procedures here, by implying that it used an either/or approach to the historicity of the gospels. In fact, Seminar members had the option of voting "undecided" (by voting "gray"), and a very large number of sayings are colored gray in *The Five Gospels*. Gray material is regarded as neither authentic nor inauthentic because the evidence is not decisive one way or the other. For a full discussion of the various shades of meaning of the Seminar's gray votes, see pp. 52–53.

3. *The Christology of Jesus* (Fortress, 1990), p. 275. See my review of this book in *Catholic Biblical Quarterly* 54 (1992), pp. 810–11.

4. *Christology*, p. 277. Here Witherington is quoting Raymond Brown.

Chapter 8

1. William Lane Craig is an outstanding evangelical apologist. His defense of the literal truth of the resurrection is wide ranging, well researched, and logically argued, though his presentation is occasionally marred by rhetoric that is insulting towards those who disagree with him. His apology is conveniently condensed in "Did Jesus Rise From the Dead?", an essay in *Jesus Under Fire*, a book in which leading evangelical scholars respond to the Jesus Seminar. Also recommended is *Will the Real Jesus Please Stand Up?*, a book based on a public debate on the resurrection between William Lane Craig and Dominic Crossan. The debate was moderated by William F. Buckley, though he shed his neutrality as a moderator to side with Craig against Crossan. This book includes the transcript of the debate and responses to it by me and Marcus Borg (who, along with Crossan, happen to be members of the Jesus Seminar). The book closes with Craig's and Crossan's concluding comments and their replies to the responses.

In adapting my response in that book for inclusion in this one, I have removed references to the Craig-Crossan debate and have reframed it to be a more general exploration of the differences between a liberal, critical approach to the resurrection and an evangelical, apologetic one. I have also added some remarks referring to Craig's reply in that book to my response.

The Craig-Crossan debate is especially interesting because both of them believe that Jesus was raised from the dead. They differ in how they interpret this belief. Craig argues that Jesus' resurrection was literal and bodily, that is, that Jesus' corpse came back to life. Crossan maintains that Jesus was raised from the dead but that this did not involve the reanimation of his corpse. Craig roundly ridicules Crossan and those like him who do not take Jesus' resurrection literally. For Craig and his fellow evangelical apologists, there is one and only one version of belief in the resurrection that is theologically valid. Craig's rhetoric is unmistakable: if you don't believe that Jesus' resurrection was literal and bodily, you have no business being a Christian.

2. Take, for example, *Jesus Under Fire*. The rhetoric of the title obviously implies that there are enemies of Jesus (i.e., the members of the Jesus Seminar) who are attacking him.

3. See the examples discussed by Maurice Bucaille in *The Bible, the Qur'an and science: the holy scriptures examined in the light of modern knowledge* (Qum: Ansariyan Publications, 1996).

4. Of course, there may be a few for whom an apology is persuasive, and for them the difference it makes in their lives is dramatic. Insiders who focus on these rare cases and ignore the rest can get the mistaken impression that apologetics is highly effective. In some cases the apologist himself came to faith this way and so knows the power of apologetics from his own experience. Converts can be very committed evangelists, missionaries, and apologists. Nevertheless, almost no Hindus, Buddhists, Jews, or Muslims (to name only some), nor atheists or agnostics will be persuaded by evangelical apologetics.

Barrett, C. K. "The Background of Mark 10:45." Pp. 1–18 in *New Testament Essays: Studies in Memory of Thomas Walter Manson*. Manchester: Manchester University Press, 1959.

Bucaille, Maurice. *The Bible, the Qur'an and science: the Holy Scriptures Examined in the Light of Modern Knowledge*. Qum: Ansariyan Publications, 1996.

Copan, Paul (ed.). *Will The Real Jesus Please Stand Up?: A Debate Between William Lane Craig and John Dominic Crossan*. Grand Rapids, Mich.: Baker Books, 1998.

Crossan, Dominic. "Why Christians Must Search for the Historical Jesus." *Bible Review* 12 (April 1996), pp. 34–38, 42.

Craig, William Lane. "Did Jesus Rise From the Dead?" Pp. 141–76, in *Jesus Under Fire: Modern Scholarship Reinvents the Historical Jesus*. Edited by Michael J. Wilkins and J. P. Moreland. Grand Rapids, Mich.: Zondervan Publishing House, 1995.

Funk, Robert W., Roy W. Hoover and the Jesus Seminar. *The Five Gospels: The Search for the Authentic Words of Jesus*. San Francisco: HarperSanFrancisco, 1993.

Funk, Robert W. and the Jesus Seminar. *The Acts of Jesus: The Search for the Authentic Deeds of Jesus*. San Francisco: HarperSanFrancisco, 1998.

Funk, Robert W. and Mahlon Smith, *The Gospel of Mark: Red Letter Edition*. Sonoma, Calif.: Polebridge Press, 1991.

Hays, Richard. "The Corrected Jesus." *First Things* (May 1994), pp. 43–48.

Hick, John. *An Interpretation of Religion*. New Haven: Yale University Press, 1989.

___, *The Metaphor of God Incarnate: Christology in a Pluralistic Age*. Louisville: Westminster John Knox Press, 1993.

Hooker, Morna. *Jesus and the Servant: The Influence of the Servant Concept of Deutero-Isaiah in the New Testament*. London: SPCK, 1959.

Johnson, Luke Timothy. "The Jesus Seminar's Misguided Quest for the Historical Jesus." *Christian Century* (January 3–10, 1996), pp. 16–22.

___, *The Real Jesus: The Misguided Quest for the Historical Jesus and the Truth of the Traditional Gospels*. San Francisco: HarperSanFrancisco, 1996.

Kee, Howard. "A Century of Quests for the Culturally Compatible Jesus." *Theology Today* 25 (April 1995), pp. 17–28.

Mack, Burton. *Who Wrote the New Testament?* San Francisco: HarperSanFrancisco, 1995.

Miller, Robert J. "Prophecy and Persecution in Luke-Acts." Ph.D. dissertation, Claremont Graduate School, 1985.

___, *Review of The Christology of Jesus by Ben Witherington. Catholic Biblical Quarterly* 54 (1992), pp. 810–11.

Miller, Robert J. (ed). *The Complete Gospels: Annotated Scholars Version.* Rev. ed. Santa Rosa, Calif: Polebridge Press. 1994.

Patterson, Stephen J. *The God of Jesus.* Philadelphia: Trinity Press International, 1998.

___, *The Gospel of Thomas and Jesus.* Sonoma, Calif., Polebridge Press, 1993.

Pearson, Birger. "The Gospel According to the Jesus Seminar." *Religion* 25 (1995), pp. 317–38.

Seeley, David. *Deconstructing the New Testament. Biblical Interpretation* 5. Leiden: Brill, 1994.

Tiede, David. *Prophecy and History in Luke-Acts.* Philadelphia: Fortress Press, 1980.

Witherington, Ben. "Battling Over the Jesus Seminar: Buyer Beware." *Bible Review* 13.2 (April 1997), pp. 23–25.

___, *The Christology of Jesus.* Minneapolis: Fortress Press, 1990.

___, *The Jesus Quest: The Third Search for the Jew from Nazareth.* Downers Grove, Ill.: InterVarsity Press, 1995.

Wright, N. T. *Jesus and the Victory of God.* Minneapolis: Fortress Press, 1996.

INDEX OF SUBJECTS AND AUTHORS

INDEX OF TEXTS DISCUSSED

This index only lists texts whose interpretations are discussed.
It does not list texts that are simply mentioned or cited.